Collecting Toy Premiums

Bread-Cereal-Radio

Prof. James L. Dundas

Schiffer Publishing Ltd

4880 Lower Valley Road, Atglen, PA 19310 USA

This book is dedicated to my brother, and all of those brothers
and sisters who were killed in Vietnam.

To Those Who Perished In Vietnam

Only memories of you my brother have I left to ease the pain,
only memories as of sunshine that is banished by the rain.
With the autumn flowers you faded and with them have gone to rest.
Forgive me in my anguish, for perhaps thou knowest best.
All in vain I try to fathom why you went to Vietnam,
was your gallant soul concealing, what we know so well today?
That you were a true American and believe in the American way,
and now have gone away.
Winter's winds will sigh in mourning, spring will bring the flowers once more,
to embellish summer's grandeur, then to die at autumn's door.
Some day God will call to me, and I will set forth,
but perhaps its a sunny morning and I will find a garden fair,
full of flowers and little children, and my brother will be there.
Smiling he will come to meet me, and I think I hear him say,
"Did you say that you had missed me? Why I haven't been away."

For Sgt. Jerry R. Dundas
Killed at Khesanh, Vietnam, on 5/5/68
from his brother Prof. James L. Dundas

Designed by John P. Cheek
Type set in AmericanaXBd BT/Humanist521 BT

ISBN: 0-7643-1123-9
Printed in China
1 2 3 4

Published by Schiffer Publishing Ltd.
4880 Lower Valley Road
Atglen, PA 19310
Phone: (610) 593-1777; Fax: (610) 593-2002
E-mail: Schifferbk@aol.com
Please visit our web site catalog at
www.schifferbooks.com
We are always looking for people to write books on new
and related subjects. If you have an idea for a book please
contact us at the above address.

This book may be purchased from the publisher.
Include $3.95 for shipping.
Please try your bookstore first.
You may write for a free catalog.

In Europe, Schiffer books are distributed by
Bushwood Books
6 Marksbury Ave.
Kew Gardens
Surrey TW9 4JF England
Phone: 44 (0) 20 8392-8585
Fax: 44 (0) 20 8392-9876
E-mail: Bushwd@aol.com
Free postage in the UK. Europe: air mail at cost

Contents

Preface

Radio and cereal premiums have been highly collectible for some time. Things that you got for free or sent for with a box top or two and a few cents now can be worth hundreds or even thousands of dollars. Although in the case of the Dick Tracy Inspector General badge, the highest rank, it took 39 box tops of Quaker Oats to get it. If you wanted the Patrol Leader badge, that was 12 more, for a grand total of 51 box tops. That's a lot of box tops for a premium! For collectible premiums, the price is only going to go up. There are only so many left. Keep in mind, however, you are not just buying toys, you're buying childhood memories, and what are they worth?

I remember the first premium that I sent for. I was eight years old. It took one box top from Kix cereal and 15 cents to get the Lone Ranger Six-Shooter gun ring. After what seemed like several hundred years worth of waiting, it finally arrived. I had near forgotten it, as it took so long to get to me. I eagerly tore into the box and there it was — the *Lone Ranger Six-Shooter gun ring*, one size fits all. I eagerly slipped it on my finger, squeezed it so it would fit just right and stared at it longingly. It did look smart, though I noticed that it stuck up quite high. After wearing it about an hour and catching it and bumping it on everything, I removed it, put it in my dresser drawer, and slipped on my Roy Rogers saddle ring instead. I never wore the Lone Ranger Six-Shooter gun ring again. But my 15 cent investment in 1948 is now worth $250.

Professor James L. Dundas

Patents and Area Codes

Patent numbers can be a great help in determining the age of an object. If a patent number ranges from 2,185,170 to 2,227,418, then the object can be no older than 1940. Keep in mind that the object may still be made today, but, usually not. A patent number expires after 17 years. Another way to tell how old an object is, is by whether or not it has an area code. Mr. Walker, the postmaster in New York, introduced a two number area code for large cities on May 6, 1943, and stopped when zip codes were introduced to the mail. Zip codes started on July 1, 1963 and have five numbers.

If it has no area or zip code, then it may be older than May 6, 1943. However, in a town or city that had only one post office from 1943 to 1963, there were no two number area or zip codes. In October 1984, "zip + four" came into being; this system has the five number zip code plus four more numbers.

So, if you have an object with a two number area code, then it was made from 1943 to 1963. If it has a zip code, then the item was made from 1963 to 1984. If you have something with five numbers then four numbers, it can be no older than October 1984.

When you find the words, Made in Japan printed on something then it was made from 1921 to 1942 and maybe to the end of World War II, August 1945. If you find "occupied Japan" printed on an item, then it was made from 1945 to 1952. Japan was occupied by the U.S. Army at the end of World War II, from late August 1945 to April 28, 1952.

Here are several examples:

John Doe Toys
123 Main Street
Detroit Mich.
An object with this address may be older than May 6, 1943.

John Doe Toys
123 Main Street
Detroit 09 Mich.
An item with this address was made from 1943 to 1963.

John Doe Toys
123 Main Street
Detroit, Mi. 48207
Any item bearing this address was made from 1963 to 1984.

John Doe Toys
123 Main Street
Detroit, MI 48207-1144
The object with this address was made from 1984 to date.

Patent Numbers

Date	Patent #	Date	Patent #	Date	Patent #	Date	Patent #	Date	Patent #	Date	Patent #
1836	1	1864	41047	1892	466315	1920	1326899	1948	2433824	1976	3930271
1837	110	1865	45685	1893	483976	1921	1354054	1949	2457797	1977	4000520
1838	546	1866	51784	1894	511744	1922	1401948	1950	2492944	1978	4065812
1839	1061	1867	60658	1895	531619	1923	1440352	1951	2536016	1979	4131952
1840	1465	1868	72959	1896	552502	1924	1478996	1952	2580379	1980	4180876
1841	1923	1869	85503	1897	574369	1925	1521590	1953	2624046	1981	4242757
1842	2413	1870	98460	1898	596467	1926	1568040	1954	2664562	1982	4308622
1843	2901	1871	110617	1899	616871	1927	1612700	1955	2698434	1983	4366579
1844	3395	1872	122304	1900	640167	1928	1654521	1956	2728913	1984	4423523
1845	3873	1873	134504	1901	664827	1929	1696897	1957	2775762	1985	4490885
1846	4348	1874	146120	1902	690385	1930	1742181	1958	2818567	1986	4562596
1847	4914	1875	158350	1903	717521	1931	1787424	1959	2868973	1987	4633526
1848	5409	1876	171641	1904	758567	1932	1839190	1960	2919443	1988	4716594
1849	5993	1877	185813	1905	778834	1933	1892663	1961	2966681	1989	4794652
1850	6961	1878	198753	1906	808618	1934	1941449	1962	3015103	1990	4890335
1851	7865	1879	211078	1907	839799	1935	1985678	1963	3070801	1991	4980927
1852	8622	1880	223211	1908	875679	1936	2026516	1964	3116487	1992	5077836
1853	9512	1881	236137	1909	908430	1937	2066309	1965	3163365	1993	5175886
1854	10358	1882	251685	1910	945010	1938	2104004	1966	3226729	1994	5274846
1855	12117	1883	269320	1911	980178	1939	2142080	1967	3295143	1995	5377359
1856	14009	1884	291016	1912	1013095	1940	2185170	1968	3360800	1996	5479658
1857	16324	1885	310163	1913	1049326	1941	2227418	1969	3419907	1997	5590420
1858	19010	1886	333494	1914	1083267	1942	2268540	1970	3487470	1998	5704062
1859	22477	1887	355291	1915	1125212	1943	2307007	1971	3551909	1999	5855021
1860	26642	1888	375720	1916	1166419	1944	2338061	1972	3633214	2000	6011000
1861	31005	1889	395305	1917	1210389	1945	2366154	1973	3707729		
1862	34045	1890	418655	1918	1251458	1946	2391856	1974	3781914		
1863	37266	1891	443987	1919	1290027	1947	2413675	1975	3858241		

If you want more information on patents, go to
www.uspto.gov or call the U.S. Patent Office: 1-800-786-9199.

Premiums

Values and Classifications

Values by condition are in three classifications: Good, Fine, and Mint.
Good: The item still works, has all its parts and shows some wear or rust.
Fine: The item still works, has all its parts and shows very little wear.
Mint: The item still works, has all its parts and is in new original condition.

The box is priced separately and is from 20% to 50% of the price of the item.

Buck Rogers

Buck Rogers was a radio program from 1932 to 1947. The sponsors were Kellogg's, Cocomalt, Cream of Wheat and Popsicle. If you wanted the Liquid Helium Water Pistol premium from Popsicle, it took 250 Popsicle wrappers.

Buck Rogers Liquid Helium Water Pistol made of copper coated steel in 1936. Scarce. $400 (Good)-$700 (Fine)-$1200 (Mint)

Buck Rogers Atomic Pistol made of copper coated steel in 1946. $200-300-500

Bond Bread

Values by condition are in three classifications: Good, Fine and Mint.

Bond bread plastic badge. $10 (Good)-$20 (Fine)-30 (Mint)

Bond bread ink blotter. $5-10-15

Bond bread flight pin back. Note that pin number 1 and 6 are not shown here. $10-15-20 each. Set of all six: $100-150-200

Bond bread ink blotter made in the late 1940s. $2-3-5

Bond bread ink blotter made in the late 1940s. $2-3-5

Bond bread ink blotter, The Lone Ranger. $15-20-25

Bread Ties

I have been told by many dealers and collectors that these bread ties, or charms, were used to keep bread wrappers closed in the 1930s. However, no one has been able to tell me which brand of bread they were used on. The prices are what I have seen them sell for in the eastern and midwestern states. Some are made of celluloid, others of plastic. They range in size from 1/2" to 1 1/2". Comic characters are worth the most.

Values by condition are in three classifications: Good, Fine and Mint.

Popeye. $10 (Good)-$20 (Fine)-$30 (Mint). Wimpy. $10-15-20

Musical players. $5-7-10 each

Sports players. $5-7-10 each

Animals. $5-7-10 each

Animals. $5-7-10 each

Animals. $5-7-10 each

Animals. $5-7-10 each

Animals. $5-7-10 each

Animals. $5-7-10 each

Miscellaneous. $5-7-10 each

A couple of Snow White's Seven
"Dwarfs." $10-20-30 each

Miscellaneous. $5-7-10 each

Miscellaneous. $5-7-10 each

Miscellaneous. $5-7-10 each

Miscellaneous. $5-7-10 each

Miscellaneous. $5-7-10 each

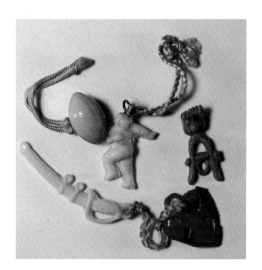

Miscellaneous. $5-7-10 each

Birds. $5-7-10 each

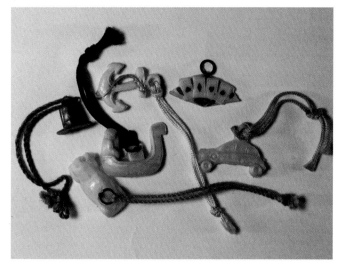

Miscellaneous. $5-7-10 each

Birds. $5-7-10 each

Rabbits. $5-7-10 each

Dogs. $5-7-10 each

Dogs. $5-7-10 each

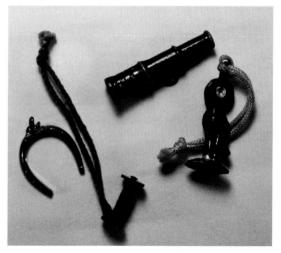

Made of metal: phone, spool, horseshoe, and telescope.
$10-20-30 each

Colonial Bread Co.

Colonial came out with the "Know Your U.S. Presidents" cards in 1976. There was one card in each loaf of bread. The object was to collect all 40 cards. The card front has a picture of the president; on the card back was a short biography. The cards are worth about $3 each in mint condition. If you have all 40, the set is worth $100 (Good)-$200 (Fine)-$300 (Mint).

Values by condition are in three classifications: Good, Fine and Mint.

 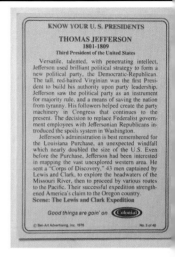

Thomas Jefferson, Third President of the United States, from 1801 to 1809. $1-2-3

 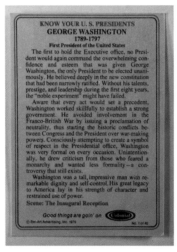

George Washington, First President of the United States, from 1789 to 1797 and back of the card. $1 (Good)-$2 (Fine)-$3 (Mint)

James Madison, Fourth President of the United States, from 1809 to 1817. $1-2-3

John Adams, Second President of the United States, from 1797 to 1801. $1-2-3

 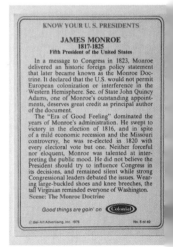

James Monroe, Fifth President of the United States, from 1817 to 1825. $1-2-3

John Quincy Adams, Sixth President of the United States, from 1825 to 1829. $1-2-3

William Henry Harrison, Ninth President of the United States, 1841. $1-2-3

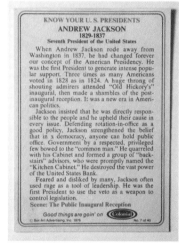

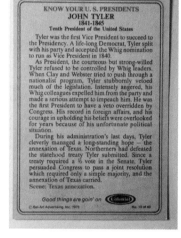

Andrew Jackson, Seventh President of the United States, from 1829 to 1837. $1-2-3

John Tyler, Tenth President of the United States, from 1841 to 1845. $1-2-3

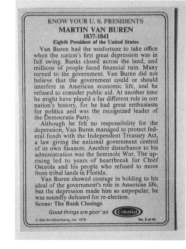

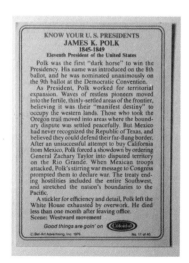

Martin Van Buren, Eighth President of the United States, from 1837 to 1841. $1-2-3

James K. Polk, Eleventh President of the United States, from 1845 to 1849. $1-2-3

Zachary Taylor, Twelfth President of the United States, from 1849 to 1850. $1-2-3

James Buchanan, Fifteenth President of the United States, from 1857 to 1861. $1-2-3

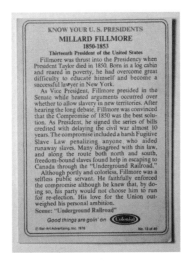

Millard Fillmore, Thirteenth President of the United States, from 1850 to 1853. $1-2-3

Abraham Lincoln, Sixteenth President of the United States, from 1861 to 1865. $1-2-3

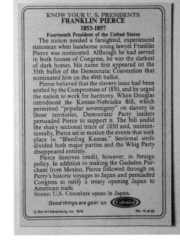

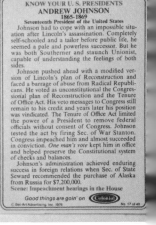

Franklin Pierce, Fourteenth President of the United States, from 1853 to 1857. $1-2-3

Andrew Johnson, Seventeenth President of the United States, from 1865 to 1869. $1-2-3

Ulysses S. Grant, Eighteenth President of the United States, from 1869 to 1877. $1-2-3

Chester A. Arthur, Twenty-first President of the United States, from 1881 to 1885. $1-2-3

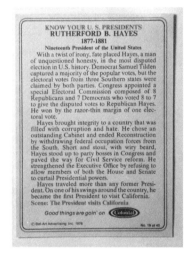

Rutherford B. Hayes, Nineteenth President of the United States, from 1877 to 1881. $1-2-3

Grover Cleveland, Twenty-second and Twenty-fourth President of the United States, from 1885 to 1889 and 1893 to 1897. $1-2-3

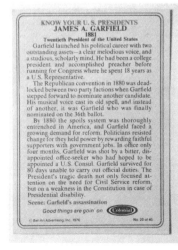

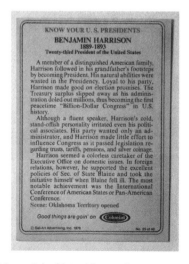

James A. Garfield, Twentieth President of the United States, 1881. $1-2-3

Benjamin Harrison, Twenty-third President of the United States, from 1889 to 1893. $1-2-3

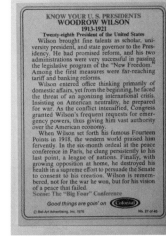

William McKinley, Twenty-fifth President of the United States, from 1897 to 1901. $1-2-3

Woodrow Wilson, Twenty-eighth President of the United States, from 1913 to 1921. $1-2-3

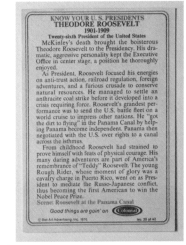

Theodore Roosevelt, Twenty-sixth President of the United States, from 1901 to 1909. $1-2-3

Warren G. Harding, Twenty-ninth President of the United States, from 1921 to 1923. $1-2-3

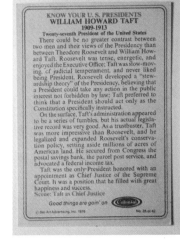
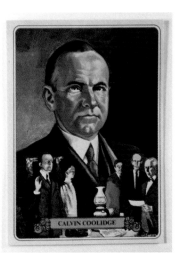
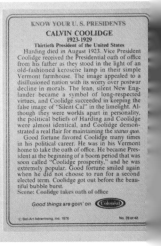

William Howard Taft, Twenty-seventh President of the United States, from 1909 to 1913. $1-2-3

Calvin Coolidge, Thirtieth President of the United States, from 1923 to 1929. $1-2-3

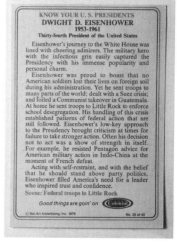

Herbert C. Hoover, Thirty-first President of the United States, from 1929 to 1933. $1-2-3

Dwight D. Eisenhower, Thirty-fourth President of the United States, from 1953 to 1961. $1-2-3

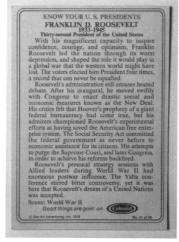

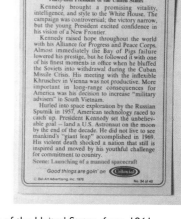

Franklin D. Roosevelt, Thirty-second President of the United States, from 1933 to 1945. $1-2-3

John F. Kennedy, Thirty-fifth President of the United States, from 1961 to 1963. $1-2-3

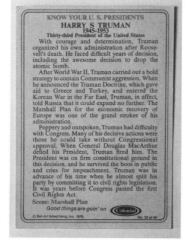

Harry S. Truman, Thirty-third President of the United States, from 1945 to 1953. $1-2-3

Lyndon B. Johnson, Thirty-sixth President of the United States, from 1963 to 1969. $1-2-3

Richard M. Nixon, Thirty-seventh President of the United States, from 1969 to 1974. $1-2-3

Gerald R. Ford, Thirty-eighth President of the United States, 1974. $1-2-3

The White House. $2-4-6

The Electoral College. $2-4-6

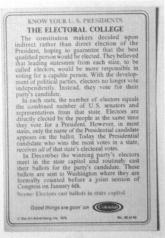

Steps In The Election Process. $2-4-6

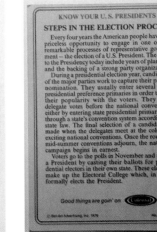

Cook Book Bread

Values by condition are in three classifications: Good, Fine and Mint.

Cook Book Bread stocking repair kit for silk stockings in the 1940s. $5 (Good)-$10 (Fine)-$15 (Mint)

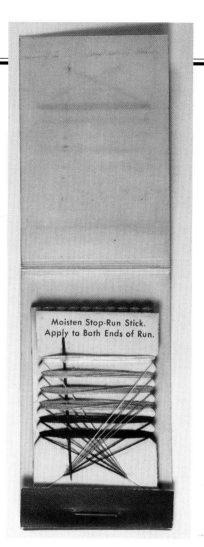

Cook Book Bread stocking repair kit, inside.

Nolde's Bread & Cakes

Values by condition are in three classifications: Good, Fine and Mint.

Nolde's Bread & Cakes Top, 1 1/2", made of tin and wood in the 1950s. $5 (Good)-10 (Fine)-15 (Mint)

Rainbo Bread

Values by condition are in three classifications: Good, Fine and Mint.

Rainbo Bread replica of a1838, $5.00 bill, 5" by 2 1/2", made in the 1940s. $5 (Good)-$10 (Fine)-$15 (Mint)

Rainbo Bread replica of a1838, $5.00 bill, 5" by 2 1/2". Back of bill.

Rainbo Bread cardboard bank. $5-7-10

Silvercup Bread

Values by condition are in three classifications: Good, Fine and Mint.

Silvercup Bread Rocky Jones Space Ranger white pin back, from a 1953 TV show. $15-25-35

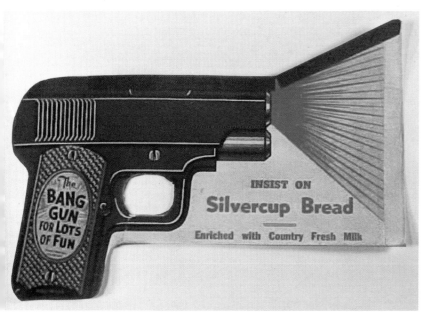

ilvercup Bread paper popper. $10 (Good)-$20 (Fine)-$30 (Mint)

Silvercup Bread Rocky Jones Space Ranger blue pin back, from a 1953 TV show (repro). $1-2-3

Sunbeam Bread

Values by condition are in three classifications: Good, Fine and Mint.

Sunbeam Bread pin back Gene Autry made in the 1950s. $15-20-30

Sunbeam Bread pencil sharpener. $5 (Good)-10 (Fine)-15 (Mint)

Sunbeam Bread pin back Davy Crockett made in the 1950s. $60-80-100

Taystee Bread

Values by condition are in three classifications: Good, Fine and Mint.

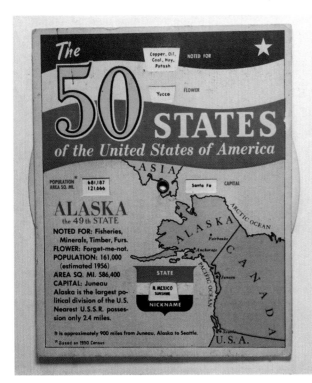

Taystee Bread The 50 States, made of cardboard in 1959, hard to find. $30 (Good)-$50 (Fine)-$70 (Mint)

Taystee Bread The 50 States, back.

Tip Top Bread

Values by condition are in three classifications: Good, Fine and Mint.

Tip Top fan, 7" tall by 10 1/2" wide when open. Made of cardboard in 1950. $20 (Good)-$30 (Fine)-$40 (Mint)

Tip Top fan front

Tip Top fan back.

Tip Top Principal Rivers of the U.S.A., 5 1/2" by 4 3/4", made of cardboard in 1946. Note: Principal Rivers on this side and Principal Bridges on other side. $25-35-45

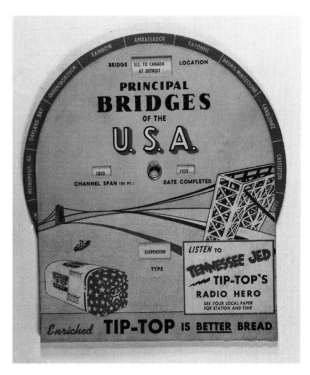

Tip Top Principal Bridges of the U.S.A., 5 1/2" by 4 3/4", made of cardboard in 1946. Note: Principal Bridges on this side, Principal Rivers on other side. $25-35-45

Tip Top Presidents of the U.S.A., 5 1/4" tall by 4 3/4" wide, made of cardboard in 1947. $20-30-40

Tip Top, Tip-Top is Tops, 1 3/8", made of plastic in 1948. $10-15-20

Tip Top sun visor, 9 1/2" by 4", made of red cardboard in 1949. $2-4-6

Tip Top Know Your U.S.A., 5 1/2" tall by 5 1/4", made of cardboard in the 1950s. $25-35-45

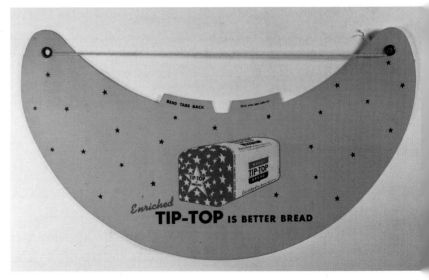

Tip Top sun visor, 9 1/2" by 4", made of yellow cardboard in 1951. $2-4-6

Tip Top sports car advertisement on one side, car on the other, 3 5/8" by 2 5/8", made of cardboard in 1954. $4-6-8

Tip Top sports car advertisement on one side, car on the other.

Tip Top The Forty-Eight States, made of cardboard in the 1940s. $15-25-35

Tip Top 1945 calendar, made of cardboard. $10-20-30

Tip Top thumb fan, made of cardboard in the 1940s. $10-15-20

Tip Top Know Your States made of cardboard, 5 1/4" high by 4 1/4" wide, made in 1953. $35-45-55

Tip Top Fan, 11 1/4" long by 6 7/8" wide, made of cardboard and wood in the 1930s. Hard to find. $40-60-80

Tip Top Know Your States made of cardboard, 5 1/4" high by 4 1/4" wide, made in 1957. $30-40-50

Tip Top Mark-it Guide made of cardboard and tin in the 1940s. $30-40-50

Tip Top Fan back.

Tip Top Official Reporter Scoop Ward News of Youth, 1 1/2" by 1 1/2", made of brass in the 1950s. $10-20-30

Wonder Bread

Values by condition are in three classifications: Good, Fine and Mint.

Wonder Bread Aircraft Spotter Dial, 5 1/4" tall by 4 1/2" wide, made of cardboard in 1943, hard to find. $60 (Good)-$70 (Fine)-$80 (Mint)

Wonder Bread Aircraft Spotter Dial back.

Wonder Bread Army-Navy Insignia Guide, 5 1/4" tall by 4 1/4" wide, made of cardboard in 1942. $30-40-50

Wonder Bread Guide to United States Warships, 4 7/8" tall by 4 1/2" wide, made of cardboard in 1943. $40-50-60

Wonder Bread Know Your Heroes Army & Navy Service Ribbons, 6 1/2" tall by 3 7/8" wide, made of cardboard in the 1940s. $30-40-50

Wonder Bread Know Your Heroes Army & Navy Service Ribbons back

Wonder Bread Guide to United States Warships back.

Wonder Bread 20 Experiments for Boys and Girls has ten experiments on each side, 5 1/4" tall by 4 5/8" wide, made of cardboard in 1946. $30-40-50

Wonder Bread Magic Tricks for Boys and Girls has ten tricks on each side, 5 1/4" tall by 4 5/8" wide, made of cardboard in 1946. $30-40-50

Wonder Bread Pencil Puzzle made of cardboard in the 1940s. $30-40-50

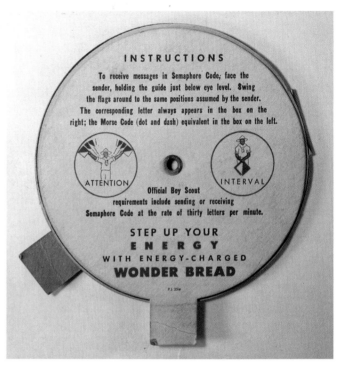

Wonder Bread Signal Code-Dial made of cardboard in the 1940s, hard to find. A cross-collectible: Boy Scouts, Wonder Bread and code collectors all want this item. $ 40-60-80

Wonder Bread Signal Code-Dial, back.

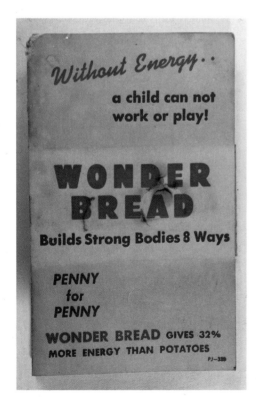

Wonder Bread Here's Your Penny Put Inside A Loaf of Bread, 5 1/4" by 3 3/8", made of cardboard in 1948. $10-15-20

Wonder Bread Here's Your Penny, back.

Wonder Bread Shopette, 1940s. $10-15-20

Wonder Bread Howdy Doody pin. When you pull the string the pin opens and says "eat Wonder Bread". This is a cross-collectible for Howdy Doody collectors and bread collectors. Made in 1950. $60-70-80

Wonder Bread bumper sticker made in the late1950s. $3-5-6

Wonder Bread Howdy Doody, 13" tall by 6" wide, made of cardboard in the 1950s. This is a cross-collectible for Howdy Doody collectors and bread collectors. Hard to find. $80-100-120

Right: Howdy Doody shake up mug top. Note the top must say Howdy Doody Cold Ovaltine Shake-up Mug, not just Cold Ovaltine.

Howdy Doody Shake-up Mug by Ovaltine. $100-125-150

Howdy Doody cup by Ovaltine. $80-90-100

Clarabell's Horn Ring from the Howdy Doody show, made in the 1950s, scarce. $250-450-600

Wonder Bread plastic rings, came in three colors: red, blue and yellow, made in the 1960s. $3-5-8

Captain Marvel

Values by condition are in three classifications: Good, Fine and Mint.

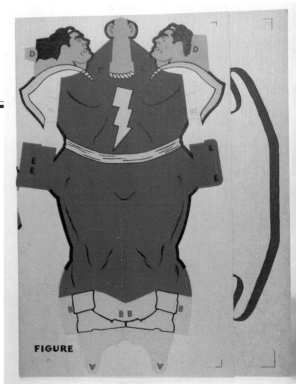

FIGURE

Captain Marvel Flying Captain Marvel paper punch-out, inside.

Captain Marvel Flying Captain Marvel paper punch-out made in 1944. $5 (Good)-$10 (Fine)-$15 (Mint)

34

Captain Marvel E.- Z. code finder, 1943. $30-40-50

Captain Marvel Jr. Ski Jump paper punch-out made in 1944. $5-10-15

Captain Midnight

Captain Midnight was a radio program in the 1940s and became a TV program in the 1950s. When Captain Midnight went to TV, the Secret Squadron designation was changed from SS to SQ . The sponsors were Skelly gasoline and Ovaltine.

Values by condition are in three classifications: Good, Fine and Mint.

Captain Midnight 1940-41 decoder manual. $50 (Good)-$100 (Fine)-$150 (Mint)

Captain Midnight 1945 decoder manual. $50-100-150

Captain Midnight 1940-41 Mystery Dial Code-O-Graph. $50-75-100

Captain Midnight 1945 Magni-Matic Code-O-Graph. $75-100-125

Captain Midnight 1942 Photomatic Code-O-Graph with photo. $75-100-125

Captain Midnight 1942 decoder manual. $50-100-150

Captain Midnight 1946 decoder manual. $50-100-150

Captain Midnight 1947 decoder manual. $75-100-125

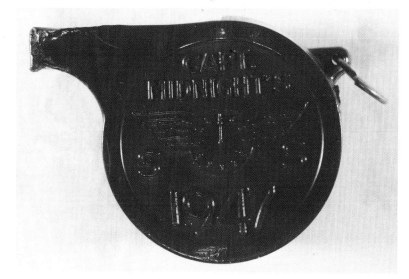

Captain Midnight 1947 Whistling Code-O-Graph. $50-75-100

Captain Midnight 1946 Mirro-Flash Code-O-Graph. $75-100-125

Captain Midnight 1947 Whistling Code-O-Graph back.

Top left: Captain Midnight 1948 decoder manual. $50-100-150

Top right: Captain Midnight 1949 decoder manual. $50-100-150

Left: Captain Midnight 1948 Mirro-Magic Code-O-Graph. $60-80-100

Right: Captain Midnight 1949 Key-O-Matic Code-O-Graph with key. $100-150-200

Bottom left: Captain Midnight 1948 Mirro-Magic Code-O-Graph back.

Bottom right: Captain Midnight 1955-56 decoder manual. $150-350-550

Captain Midnight 1955-56 membership card. $50-80-125

Captain Midnight 1955-56 Plastic Decoder. $150-300-500

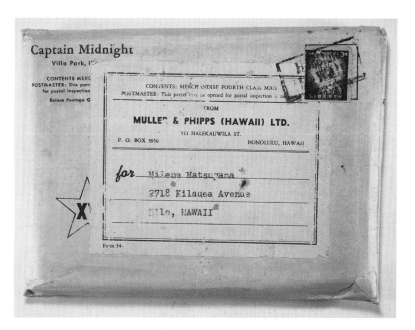

Captain Midnight 1957 mailer. $150-250-350

Captain Midnight 1955-56 Plastic Decoder, back.

Captain Midnight 1957 decoder manual. $100-250-400

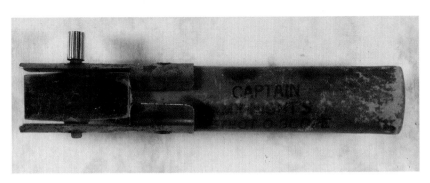

Captain Midnight Five-way Detect-O-Scope, 1940-41. $40-60-80

Captain Midnight 1957 handbook. $50-75-100

Captain Midnight 1947 embossed Shake-up Mug, orange with a blue top. $50-100-150

Captain Midnight 1957 Silver Dart SQ plastic Decoder. $150-250-350

Captain Midnight 1957 Silver Dart SQ plastic Decoder, back.

Captain Midnight 1947 embossed Shake-up Mug, embossed blue top.

Captain Midnight 1953 Mug. $40-50-60

Captain Midnight 1939 Mysto-Magic weather forecasting flight wings. $50-75-100

Captain Midnight 15th anniversary Shake-up Mug, 1957 red with a blue top. $50-75-100

Captain Midnight 1940-41 Spinner Membership, made of brass. $20-30-40. Note the reproductions are made of pewter or have a small "r under the S" in Skelly. $2-3-4

Captain Midnight 1940-41 Spinner Membership back.

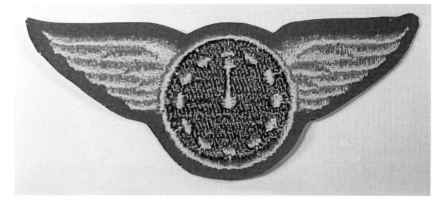

Captain Midnight 1943 shoulder patch. $50-100-150

Captain Midnight 15th anniversary Shake-up Mug, blue top.

Captain Midnight 1942 Sliding Secret Compartment ring. $100-150-200

Captain Midnight 1942 Look Around ring. $100-150-200

Values by condition are in three classifications: Good, Fine and Mint.

Captain Video flying saucer ring, very scarce, complete. $1000-1500-2000

Captain Video radio scillograph. This is only one of the set. Battery operated, made of bakelite and cardboard, made in the early 1950s, very hard to find. One unit. $300 (Good)-$400 (Fine)-$500 (Mint). A complete set. $1000 (Good)-$1500 (Fine)-$2000 (Mint)

Captain Video Mysto-Coder made in 1951, very scarce. $500-1000-1500

Captain Video Mysto-Coder back.

Captain Video paper cutout made of cardboard, made in the early 1950s. $20-30-40

Captain Video Mysto-Coder with removed red stone to show a picture of Capt. Video.

Kellogg's Cereal

Values by condition are in three classifications: Good, Fine and Mint.

Kellogg's Corn Flakes Jet-drive whistle locos made of plastic in 1950. These items came in blue, black, red and green. $20 (Good)-$30 (Fine)-$40 (Mint)

Kellogg's Cereal Walkie Talkie set, made of plastic in the 1950s. $60-80-100

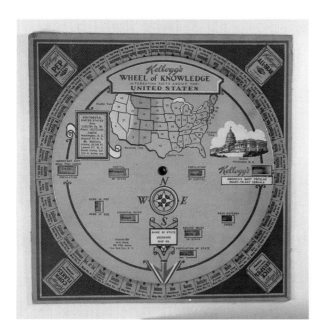

Kellogg's Wheel of Knowledge made of cardboard in the 1950s. $10-20-30

Kellogg's Cereal Walkie Talkie set original shipping box. $10-20-30

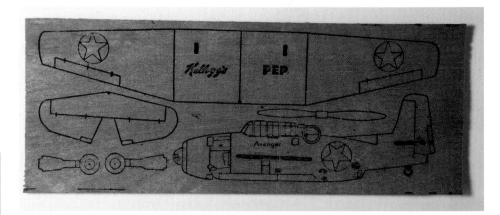

Kellogg's Pep Model War Plane No. 19 Grumman "Avenger."

Kellogg's Pep Model War Plane Series. There were a total of 20 in the series; this is No. 19, a Grumman "Avenger," made of wood in 1943, hard to find. $40-60-80

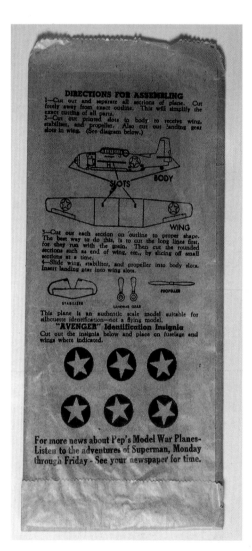

Kellogg's Pep Model War Plane No. 19 Grumman "Avenger."

Kellogg's Pep Model War Plane Series. There were a total of 20 in the series, this is No. 9, a Haeker "Hurricane," made of wood in 1943, hard to find. $40-60-80

44

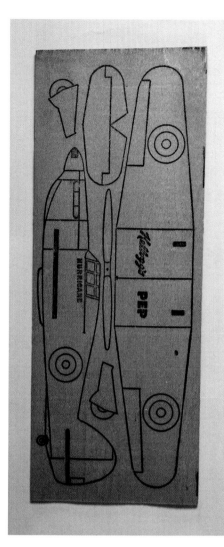

Kellogg's Pep Model War Plane No. 9 Haeker "Hurricane."

Kellogg's Pep Model War Plane No. 21 Curtiss "Seagull." $40-60-80

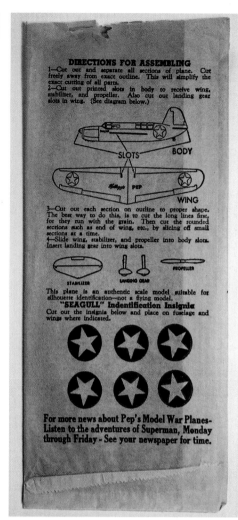

Kellogg's Pep Model War Plane No. 21 Curtiss "Seagull."

Kellogg's Pep Model War Plane No. 21 Curtiss "Seagull."

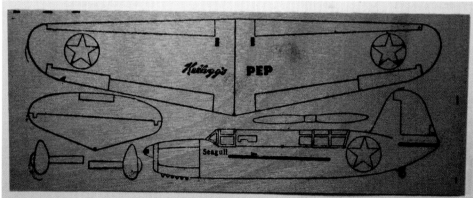

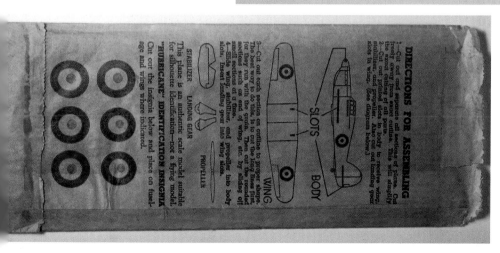

Kellogg's Pep Model War Plane No. 9 Haeker "Hurricane."

Kellogg's Kutouts game "Jump" made in the 1950s. $5-10-15

Kellogg's Kutouts "Jeep" made in the 1950s. $5-10-15

Kellogg's Pep Pin, 402nd Bombardment Squadron, made of tin in 1943. $5-10-15

Kellogg's Pep Pin, Navy Patrol Squadron 23, made of tin in 1943. $5-10-15

Kellogg's Pep Pin, 48th Bombardment Squadron, made of tin in 1943. $5-10-15

Kellogg's Pep Pin, back.

Kellogg's Pep Pin, 471st Bombardment Squadron, made of tin in 1943. $5-10-15

Kellogg's Pep Pin, Daddy Warbucks, made in 1946. $5-10-15

Kellogg's Pep Pin, Radio Orphan Annie, made in 1945. $10-15-20

Kellogg's Pep Pin, Kayo, made in 1945. $3-6-10

Kellogg's Pep Pin, Shadow, made in 1945. $3-6-10

Kellogg's Pep Pin, Sandy, made in 1945. $5-10-15

Kellogg's Pep Pin, Harold Teen, made in 1945. $3-6-10

Kellogg's Pep Pin, Smokey Stoyer, made in 1945. $3-6-10

Kellogg's Pep Pin, Dick Tracy, made in 1945. $20-30-40

Kellogg's Pep Pin, Uncle Walt, made in 1945. $3-6-10

Kellogg's Pep Pin, Herby, made in 1945. $3-6-10

Kellogg's Pep Pin, Superman, made in 1945. $20-30-40

Kellogg's Pep Pin, Nina, made in 1945. $3-6-10

Some of the Additional Kellogg's Pep Pins:

Moon Mullins, 1945	$3-6-10
Skeezix, 1945	$3-6-10
Emmy, 1945	$3-6-10
Marine Fighter Squadron VM F 224, 1940s	$10-15-20
Marine Bombing Squad 443, 1940s	$10-15-20
Navy Stagron 14, 1940s	$10-15-20
Navy Bombing Squadron 12, 1940s	$10-15-20

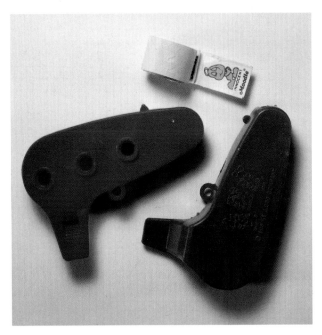

Kellogg's Rice Krispies Snap, Crackle, Pop, whistle with stick-ons packaged inside the whistle, made in 1985. $5-10-15

Kellogg's Binoculars made of cardboard and plastic in 1988. $10-20-30

Kellogg's Rice Krispies Snap, Crackle, Pop, Duncan Yo Yo made in 1989. $5-10-15

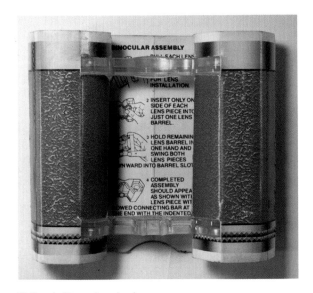

Kellogg's Binoculars, back.

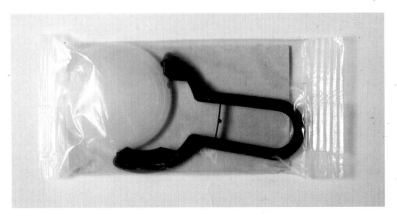

Kellogg's Disk Launcher, 5" long x 2 1/2" wide, made in 1993. $1-3-5

Kellogg's Rice Krispies Atom Sub toy, 1954-1955, made of plastic. $15-20-25

Kellogg's Corn Flakes Dragnet Whistle made of plastic in 1955. $5-10-15

Kellogg's The Apple Jacks Kids decoder made of plastic in 1983. $10-20-30

Kellogg's Corn Flakes Dragnet Whistle made of plastic with a paper label. $10-15-20

Kellogg's Rice Krispies PT Boat, baking powder powered, made of plastic in 1955. $20-40-60

Kellogg's Singing Lady Mother Goose Action Circus. $3-7-10

49

Kellogg's Histories of Flight: there were two sets with 150 cards in each set. These cards were made in the 1950s.

Kellogg's Histories of Flight #15 Channel Crossing. $1-2-3

Kellogg's ALL-WHEAT
2ND SET OF 150 CARDS
CHANNEL CROSSING
No. 15 in a Series of 15
Histories of Flight

Bleriot, a Frenchman, was the first man to make an international flight, when he crossed the English Channel in July, 1909. He made the flight from Calais to Dover, a distance of 25 miles in 37 minutes! Before he started his monoplane, this flyer, who had an injured foot, said, "If I cannot walk, I will show the world I can fly." The English gave him a great ovation. A monument has been erected where he landed near Dover.

Blériot, un Français, effectua la première traversée de la Manche en avion. En 1909, il vola 25 milles en 37 minutes.

TRAIN RIGHT...EAT RIGHT...BE A WINNER!

Kellogg's Histories of Flight #15 Channel Crossing, back.

Kellogg's Histories of Flight #14 Farman's Flight. $1-2-3

Kellogg's Histories of Flight #10 Invasion Balloon. $1-2-3

Kellogg's Histories of Flight #12 Glider Parachute. $1-2-3

Kellogg's Histories of Flight #9 First
Parachute Jump. $1-2-3

Kellogg's Histories of Flight #6 Montgolfier's
"Balon." $1-2-3

Kellogg's Histories of Flight #7 Franconville
Balloon. $1-2-3

Kellogg's Histories of Flight #8 Crosbie's
Chariot. $1-2-3

Kellogg's Histories of Flight #4 Lana's Flying
Boat. $1-2-3

Kellogg's Bonkers makes a siren sound. This item was made for a bicycle in 1995. *Courtesy of Dorothy Schillinger.* $5-10-15

Kix Cereal

Values by condition are in three classifications: Good, Fine and Mint.

Kix Cereal plastic airplanes made in 1946, P-38. $3-5-8

Kix Cereal plastic airplanes made in 1946, B-25. $3 (Good)-$5 (Fine)-$8 (Mint)

Kix Cereal plastic airplanes made in 1946, B-24. $3-5-8

Kix Cereal plastic airplanes made in 1946, B-17. $3-5-8

Kix Cereal plastic airplanes made in 1946, Thunderbolt. $3-5-8

Kix Cereal plastic airplanes made in 1946, Corsair. $3-5-8

Kix Cereal Rocket-To-The-Moon ring, made in 1951. This ring came with three rockets and is very hard to find. $500-1000-1500

Straight Arrow was on the radio from 1948 to 1954. Straight Arrow was really Steve Adams, who would go to his secret cave and change to the "Injun" Straight Arrow. The sponsor was Nabisco Shredded Wheat, which from 1949 to 1952 had Straight Arrow Injun-Uity Manual spacer cards to separate the shredded wheat biscuits. There were 12 cereal biscuits to a box with 3 separator cards. There were four sets of 36 Straight Arrow Injun-uities that made a book. There were four books with 36 cards to a book. Book 1 was issued in 1949, book 2 in 1950, book 3 in 1951, and book 4 in 1952.

Values by condition are in three classifications: Good, Fine and Mint.

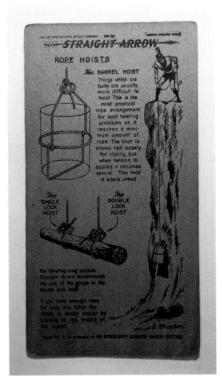

Straight Arrow Book 1 #3. $1-2-3

Straight Arrow Book 1 cover. $1 (Good)-$2 (Fine)-$3 (Mint)

Straight Arrow Book 1 #2. $1-2-3

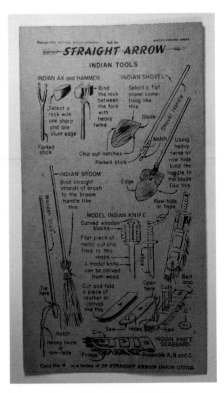

Straight Arrow Book 1 #4. $1-2-3

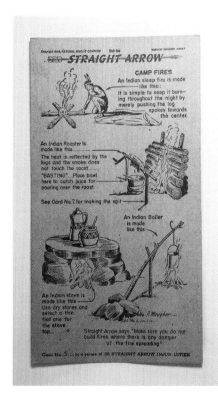

Straight Arrow Book 1 #5. $1-2-3

Straight Arrow Book 1 #7. $1-2-3

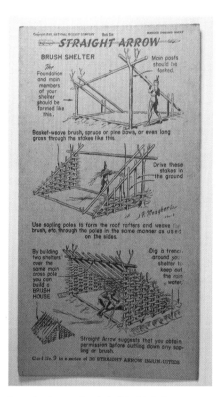

Straight Arrow Book 1 #9. $1-2-3

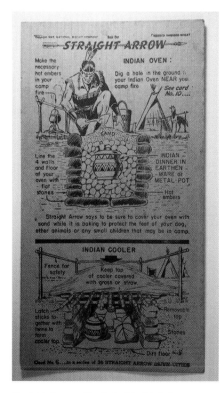

Straight Arrow Book 1 #6. $1-2-3

Straight Arrow Book 1 #8. $1-2-3

Straight Arrow Book 1 #10. $1-2-3

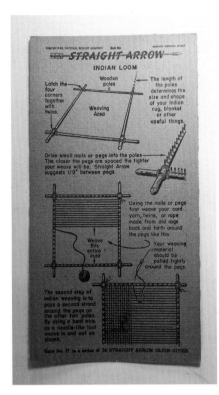

Straight Arrow Book 1 #11. $1-2-3

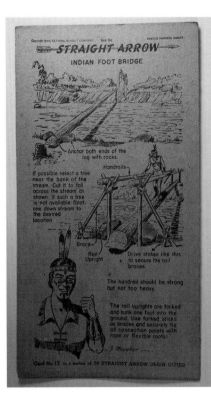

Straight Arrow Book 1 #13. $1-2-3

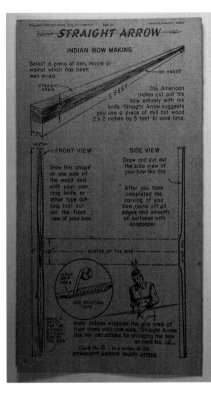

Straight Arrow Book 1 #15. $1-2-3

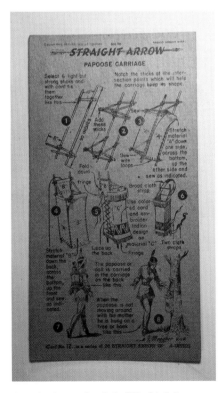

Straight Arrow Book 1 #12. $1-2-3

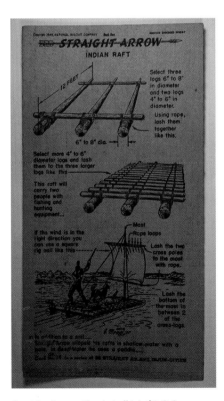

Straight Arrow Book 1 #14. $1-2-3

Straight Arrow Book 1 #16. $1-2-3

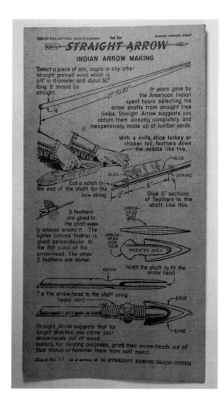

Straight Arrow Book 1 #17. $1-2-3

Straight Arrow Book 1 #19. The Announcement is very hard to find. $20-30-40

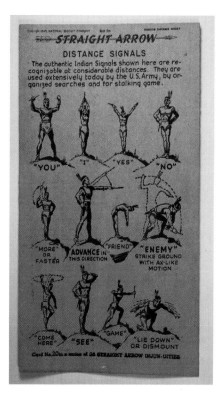

Straight Arrow Book 1 #20. $1-2-3

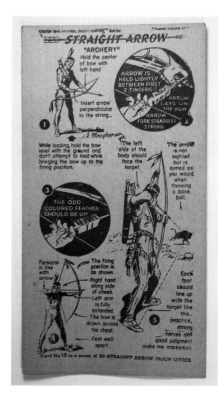

Straight Arrow Book 1 #18. $1-2-3

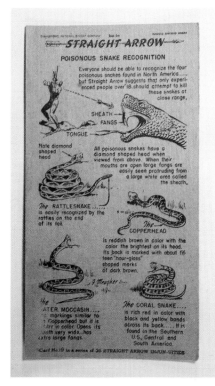

Straight Arrow Book 1 #19. $3-6-9

Straight Arrow Book 1 #21. $1-2-3

Straight Arrow Book 1 #22. $1-2-3

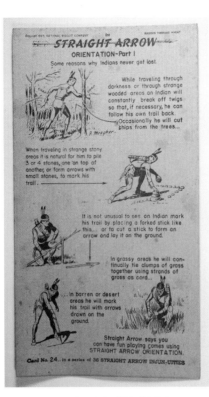

Straight Arrow Book 1 #24. $1-2-3

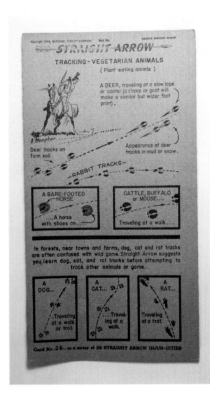

Straight Arrow Book 1 #26. $1-2-3

Straight Arrow Book 1 #23. $1-2-3

Straight Arrow Book 1 #25. $1-2-3

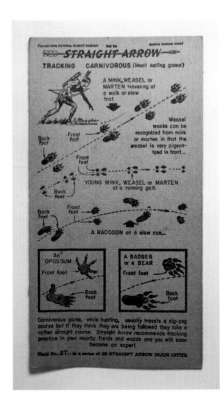

Straight Arrow Book 1 #27. $1-2-3

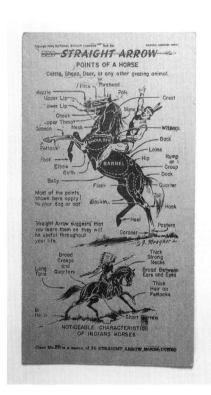

Straight Arrow Book 1 #28. $1-2-3

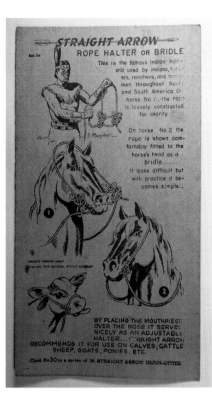

Straight Arrow Book 1 #30. $1-2-3

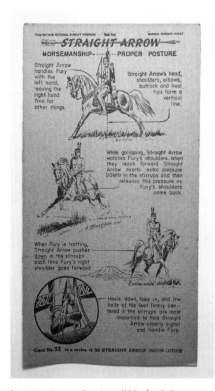

Straight Arrow Book 1 #32. $1-2-3

Straight Arrow Book 1 #29. $1-2-3

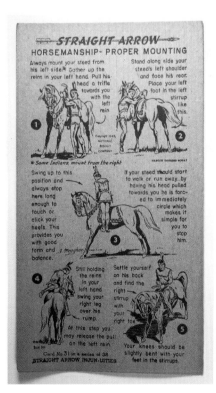

Straight Arrow Book 1 #31. $1-2-3

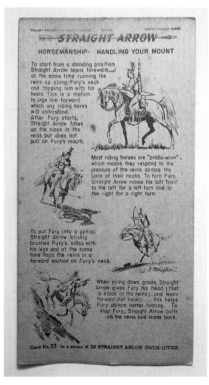

Straight Arrow Book 1 #33. $1-2-3

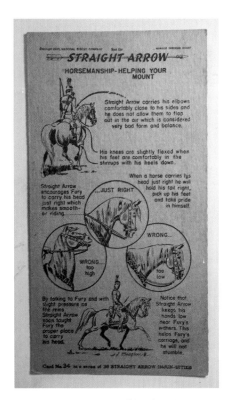

Straight Arrow Book 1 #34. $1-2-3

Straight Arrow Book 1 #36. $1-2-3. Complete set of book 1 pages. $50-100-150

Straight Arrow Book 2 #2. $1-2-3

Straight Arrow Book 1 #35. $1-2-3

Straight Arrow Book 2 cover. $1-2-3

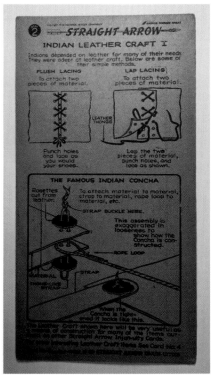

Straight Arrow Book 2 #3. $1-2-3

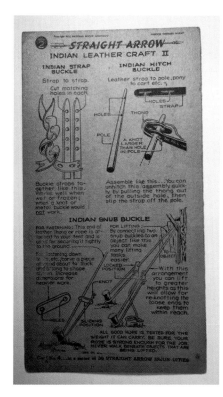

Straight Arrow Book 2 #4. $1-2-3

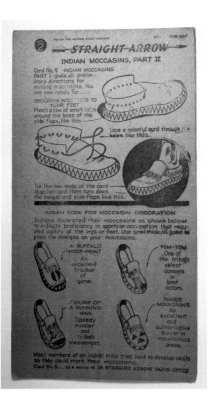

Straight Arrow Book 2 #6. $1-2-3

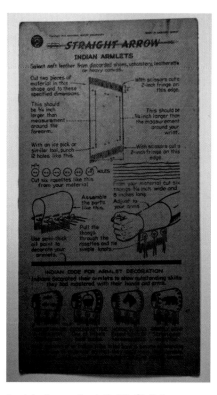

Straight Arrow Book 2 #8. $1-2-3

Straight Arrow Book 2 #5. $1-2-3

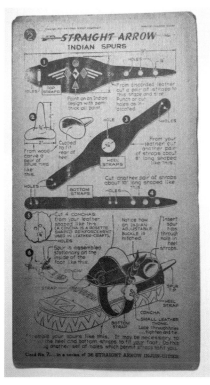

Straight Arrow Book 2 #7. $1-2-3

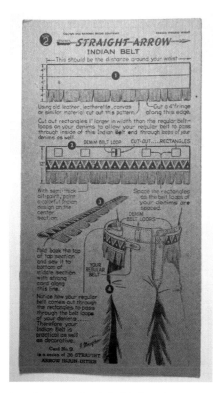

Straight Arrow Book 2 #9. $1-2-3

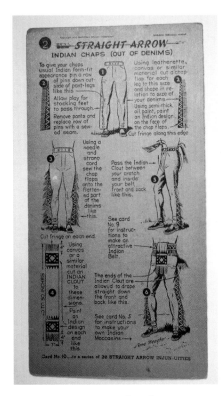

Straight Arrow Book 2 #10. $1-2-3

Straight Arrow Book 2 #12. $1-2-3

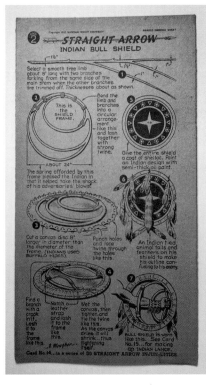

Straight Arrow Book 2 #14. $1-2-3

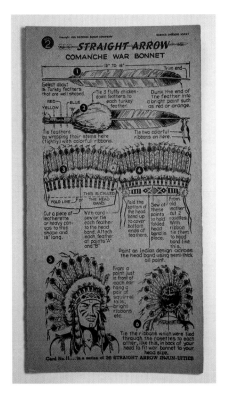

Straight Arrow Book 2 #11. $1-2-3

Straight Arrow Book 2 #13. $1-2-3

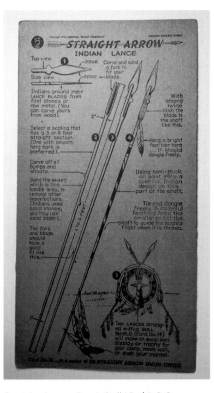

Straight Arrow Book 2 #15. $1-2-3

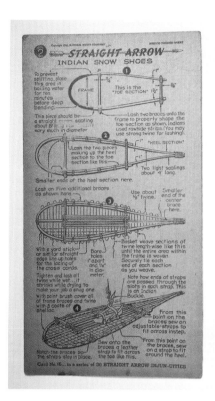

Straight Arrow Book 2 #16. $1-2-3

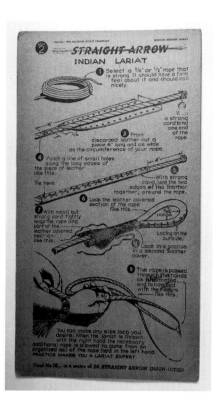

Straight Arrow Book 2 #18. $1-2-3

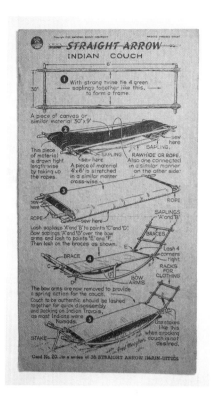

Straight Arrow Book 2 #20. $1-2-3

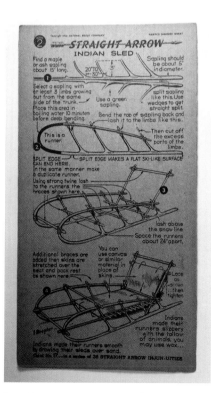

Straight Arrow Book 2 #17. $1-2-3

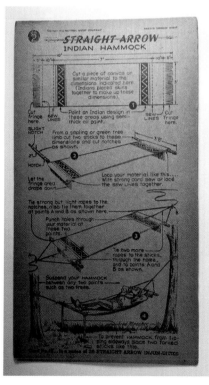

Straight Arrow Book 2 #19. $1-2-3

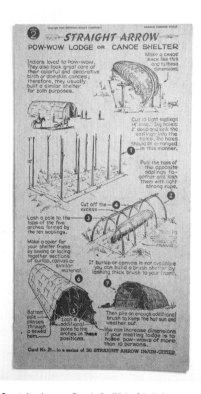

Straight Arrow Book 2 #21. $1-2-3

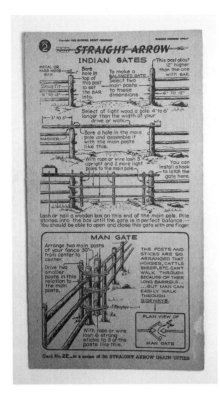

Straight Arrow Book 2 #22. $1-2-3

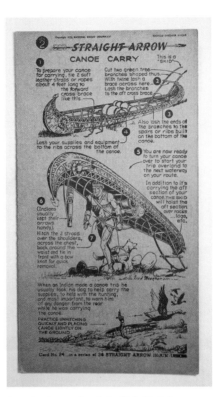

Straight Arrow Book 2 #24. $1-2-3

Straight Arrow Book 2 #26. $1-2-3

Straight Arrow Book 2 #23. $1-2-3

Straight Arrow Book 2 #25. $1-2-3

Straight Arrow Book 2 #27. $1-2-3

Straight Arrow Book 2 #28. $1-2-3

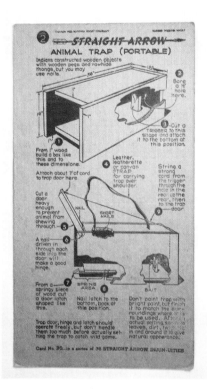

Straight Arrow Book 2 #30. $1-2-3

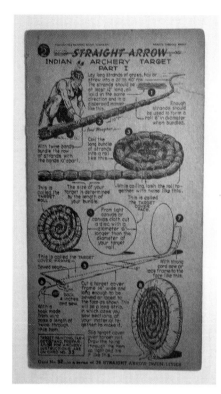

Straight Arrow Book 2 #32. $1-2-3

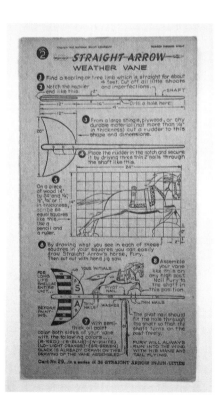

Straight Arrow Book 2 #29. $1-2-3

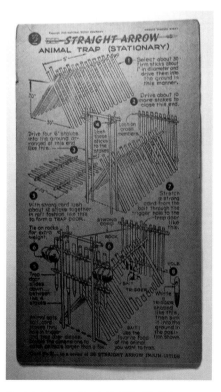

Straight Arrow Book 2 #31. $1-2-3

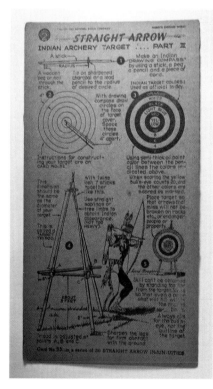

Straight Arrow Book 2 #33. $1-2-3

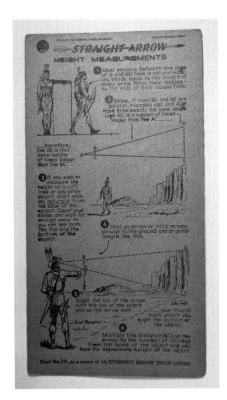

Straight Arrow Book 2 #34. $1-2-3

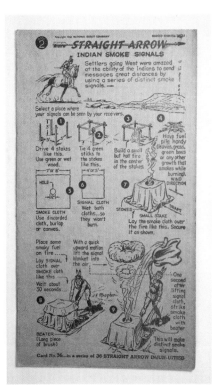

Straight Arrow Book 2 #36. $1-2-3.
Complete set of book 2 pages. $50-80-120

Straight Arrow Book 3 #2. $1-2-3

Straight Arrow Book 2 #35. $1-2-3

Straight Arrow Book 3 cover. $1-2-3

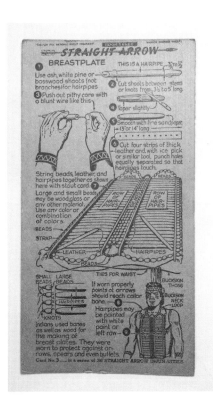

Straight Arrow Book 3 #3. $1-2-3

Straight Arrow Book 3 #4. $1-2-3

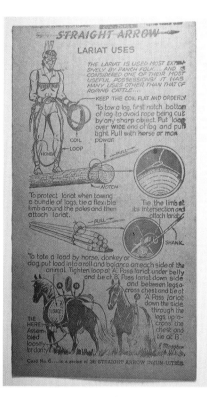

Straight Arrow Book 3 #6. $1-2-3

Straight Arrow Book 3 #8. $1-2-3

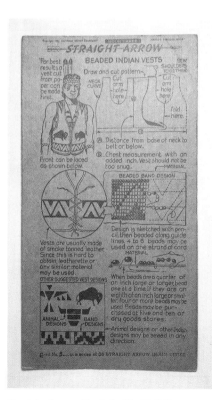

Straight Arrow Book 3 #5. $1-2-3

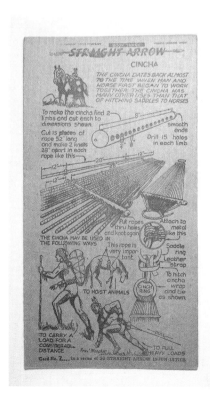

Straight Arrow Book 3 #7. $1-2-3

Straight Arrow Book 3 #9. $1-2-3

Straight Arrow Book 3 #10. $1-2-3

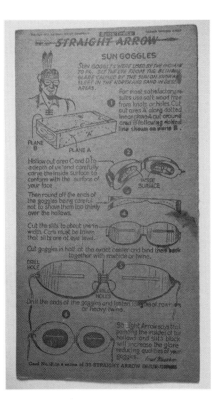

Straight Arrow Book 3 #12. $1-2-3

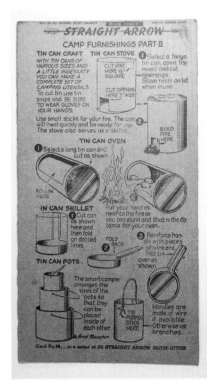

Straight Arrow Book 3 #14. $1-2-3

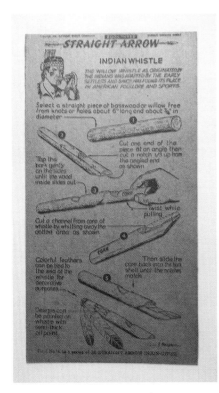

Straight Arrow Book 3 #11. $1-2-3

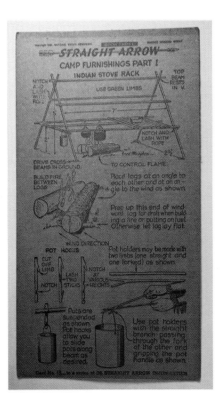

Straight Arrow Book 3 #13. $1-2-3

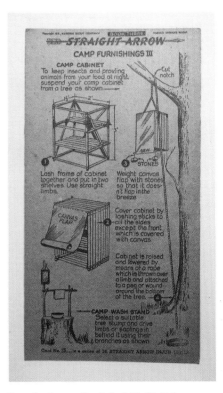

Straight Arrow Book 3 #15. $1-2-3

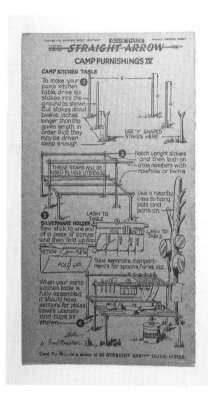

Straight Arrow Book 3 #16. $1-2-3

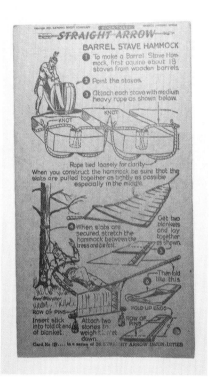

Straight Arrow Book 3 #18. $1-2-3

Straight Arrow Book 3 #20. $1-2-3

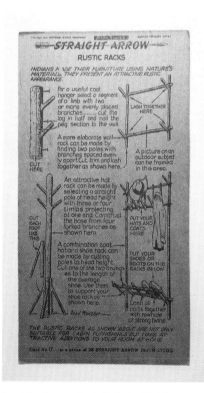

Straight Arrow Book 3 #17. $1-2-3

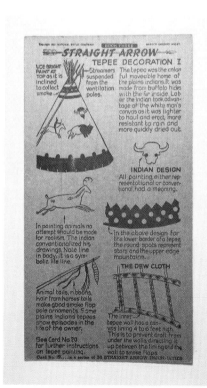

Straight Arrow Book 3 #19. $1-2-3

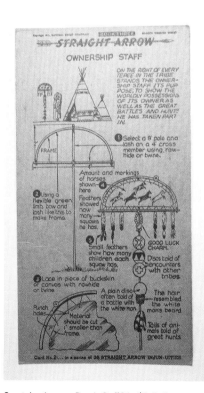

Straight Arrow Book 3 #21. $1-2-3

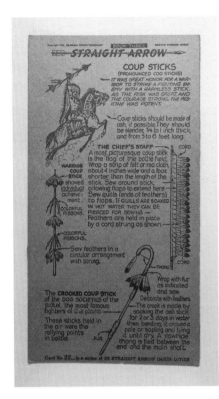

Straight Arrow Book 3 #22. $1-2-3

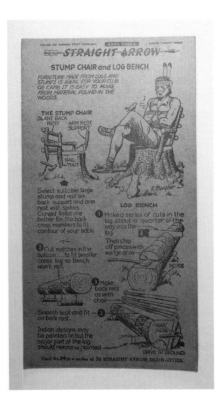

Straight Arrow Book 3 #24. $1-2-3

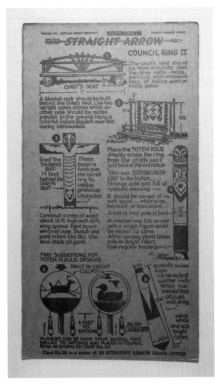

Straight Arrow Book 3 #26. $1-2-3

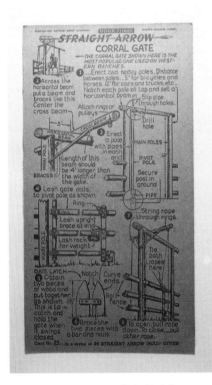

Straight Arrow Book 3 #23. $1-2-3

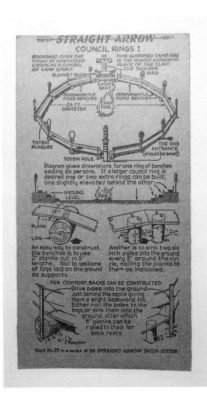

Straight Arrow Book 3 #25. $1-2-3

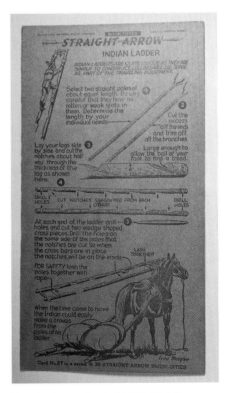

Straight Arrow Book 3 #27. $1-2-3

Straight Arrow Book 3 #28. $1-2-3

Straight Arrow Book 3 #30. $1-2-3

Straight Arrow Book 3 #32. $1-2-3

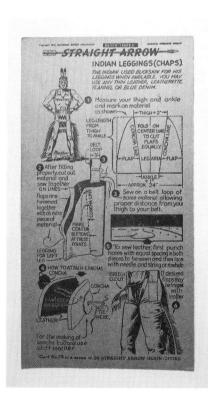

Straight Arrow Book 3 #29. $1-2-3

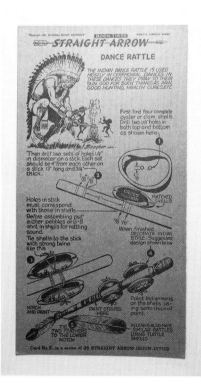

Straight Arrow Book 3 #31. $1-2-3

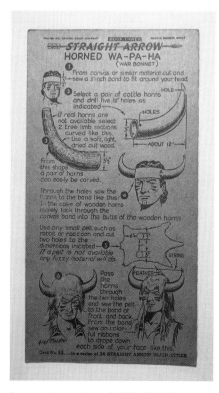

Straight Arrow Book 3 #33. $1-2-3

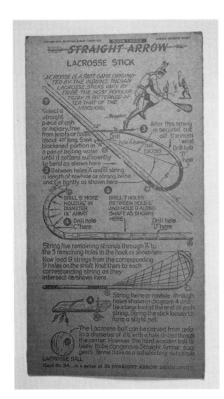

Straight Arrow Book 3 #34. $1-2-3

Straight Arrow Book 3 #36. $1-2-3.
Complete set of book 3 pages. $50-80-120

Straight Arrow Book 4 #2. $1-2-3

Straight Arrow Book 3 #35. $1-2-3

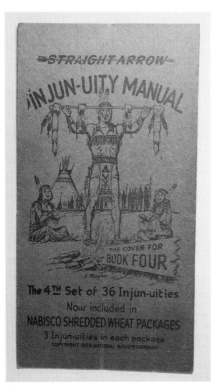

Straight Arrow Book 4 cover. $1-2-3

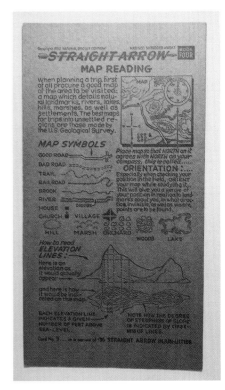

Straight Arrow Book 4 #3. $1-2-3

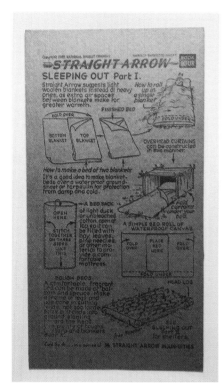

Straight Arrow Book 4 #4. $1-2-3

Straight Arrow Book 4 #6. $1-2-3

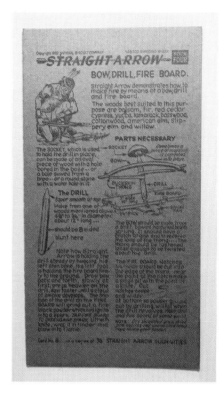

Straight Arrow Book 4 #8. $1-2-3

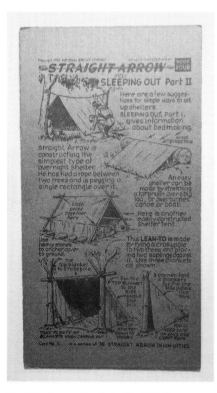

Straight Arrow Book 4 #5. $1-2-3

Straight Arrow Book 4 #7. $1-2-3

Straight Arrow Book 4 #9. $1-2-3

Straight Arrow Book 4 #10. $1-2-3

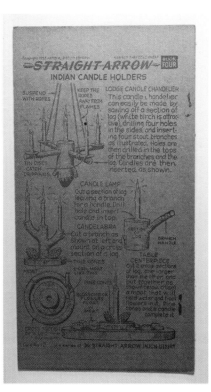

Straight Arrow Book 4 #12. $1-2-3

Straight Arrow Book 4 #14. $1-2-3

Straight Arrow Book 4 #11. $1-2-3

Straight Arrow Book 4 #13. $1-2-3

Straight Arrow Book 4 #15. $1-2-3

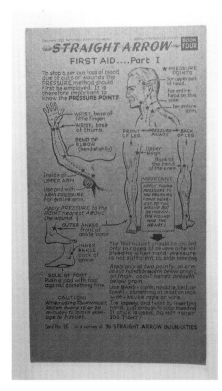

Straight Arrow Book 4 #16. $1-2-3

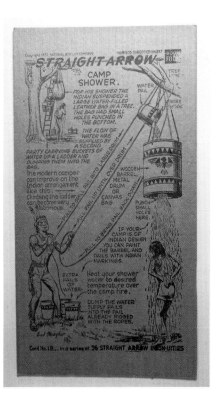

Straight Arrow Book 4 #18. $1-2-3

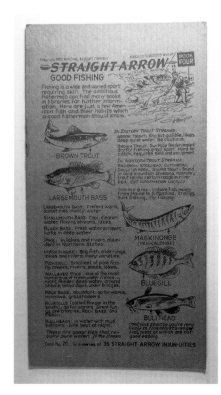

Straight Arrow Book 4 #20. $1-2-3

Straight Arrow Book 4 #17. $1-2-3

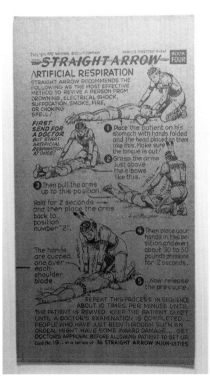

Straight Arrow Book 4 #19. $1-2-3

Straight Arrow Book 4 #21. $1-2-3

Straight Arrow Book 4 #22. $1-2-3

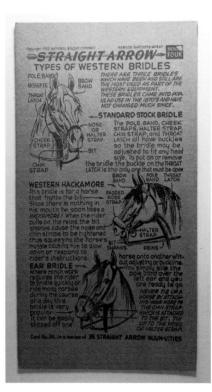

Straight Arrow Book 4 #24. $1-2-3

Straight Arrow Book 4 #26. $1-2-3

Straight Arrow Book 4 #23. $1-2-3

Straight Arrow Book 4 #25. $1-2-3

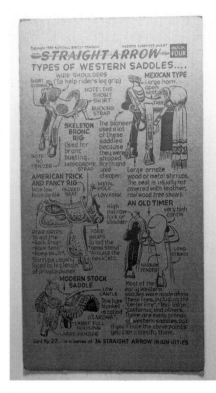

Straight Arrow Book 4 #27. $1-2-3

Straight Arrow Book 4 #28. $1-2-3

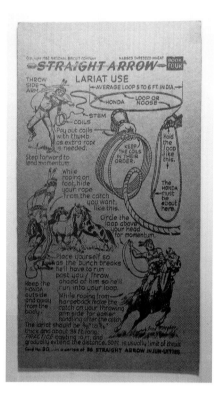

Straight Arrow Book 4 #30. $1-2-3

Straight Arrow Book 4 #32. $1-2-3

Straight Arrow Book 4 #29. $1-2-3

Straight Arrow Book 4 #31. $1-2-3

Straight Arrow Book 4 #33. $1-2-3

77

Straight Arrow Book 4 #34. $1-2-3

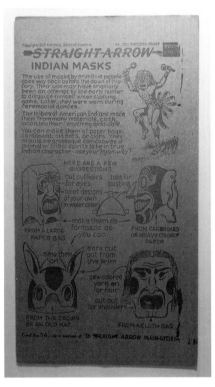

Straight Arrow Book 4 #36. $1-2-3.
Complete set of book 4 pages. $50-80-125

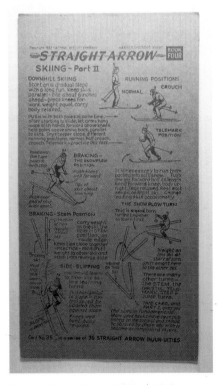

Straight Arrow Book 4 #35. $1-2-3

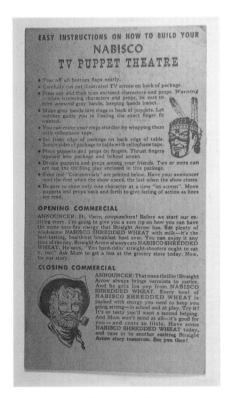

Straight Arrow TV Puppet Theater separator card, hard to find. $10-20-30

Straight Arrow Cut Out Characters separator card, hard to find. $10-20-30

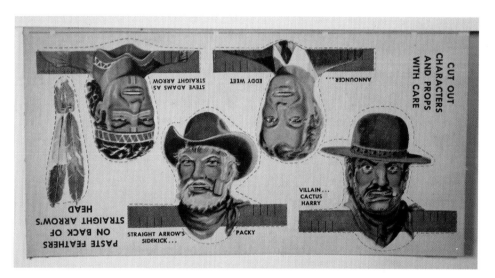

Straight Arrow Cut Out Characters separator card, hard to find. $10-20-30

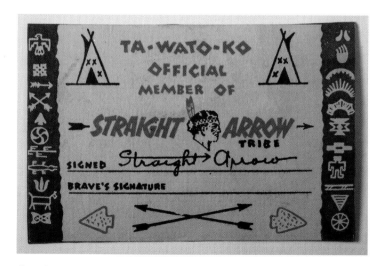

Straight Arrow Ta-Wato-Ko official member card, hard to find. $20-40-60

Straight Arrow cloth patch, hard to find. $40-60-80

Straight Arrow kerchief made in 1949. $40-60-80

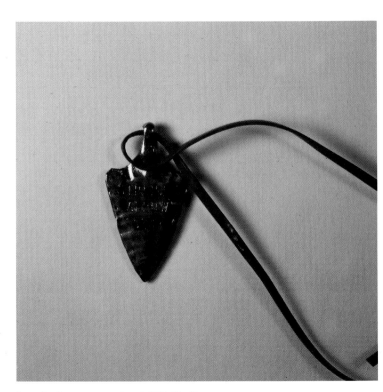

Straight Arrow arrow head. $20-30-40

Straight Arrow Golden Nugget Ring, with a photo of the inside of the Golden Nugget Cave visible through the hole in the nugget. $100-200-300

Straight Arrow Indian head band made of paper. $30-40-50

Rin Tin Tin

Values by condition are in three classifications: Good, Fine and Mint.

Nabisco Rin Tin Tin Sweat Shirt, Copyright 1956. $3 (Good)-$7 (Fine)-$10 (Mint)

Nabisco Rin Tin Tin Cavalry Uniform, Copyright 1956. $3-7-10

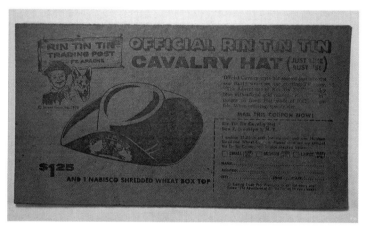

Nabisco Rin Tin Tin Cavalry Hat, Copyright 1956. $3-7-10

Nabisco Rin Tin Tin T-Shirt, Copyright 1956. $3-7-10

Nabisco Rin Tin Tin Cavalry Mess Kit, Copyright 1956. $3-7-10

Nabisco Rin Tin Tin Stuffed "Rinty" Dog, Copyright 1956. $3-7-10

Nabisco Rin Tin Tin Beanie, Copyright 1956. $3-7-10

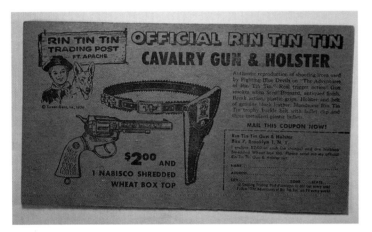

Nabisco Rin Tin Tin Cavalry Gun & Holster, Copyright 1956. $3-7-10

Nabisco Rin Tin Tin Cavalry Belt, Copyright 1956. $3-7-10

Nabisco Rin Tin Tin Cavalry Bugle, Copyright 1956. $3-7-10

Nabisco Rin Tin Tin Membership Kit, Copyright 1956. $3-7-10

Toytown

There were 36 cards to the Toytown set. You were to color each structure using the color guide and then cut them out and put them together. A complete set is valued as follows: $50 (Good)-$75 (Fine)-$100 (Mint).

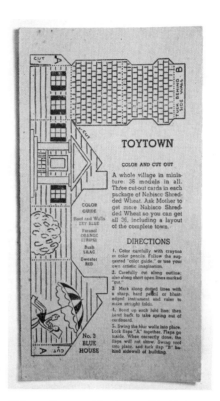

Nabisco Toytown blue house #3. $1-2-3

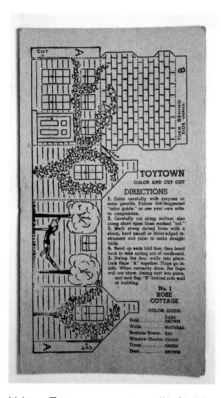

Nabisco Toytown rose cottage #1. $1-2-3

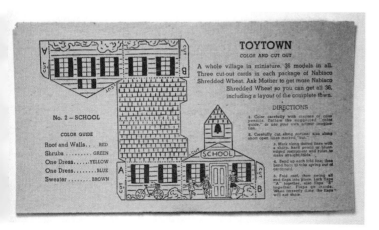

Nabisco Toytown school #2. $1-2-3

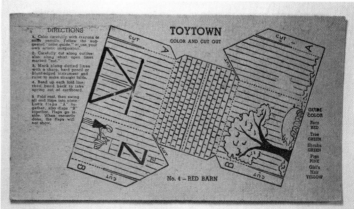

Nabisco Toytown red barn #4. $1-2-3

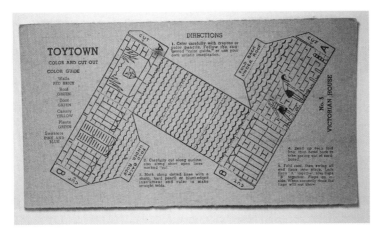

Nabisco Toytown Victorian house #5. $1-2-3

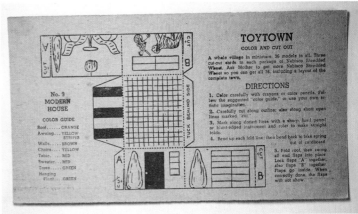

Nabisco Toytown modern house #9. $1-2-3

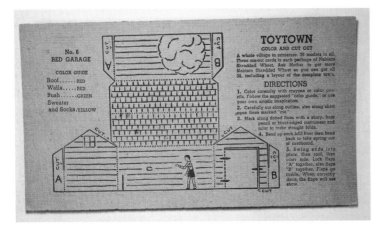

Nabisco Toytown red garage #6. $1-2-3

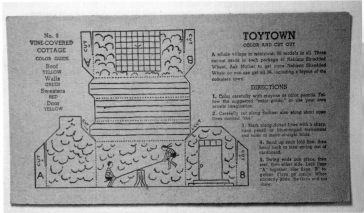

Nabisco Toytown vine-covered cottage #8. $1-2-3

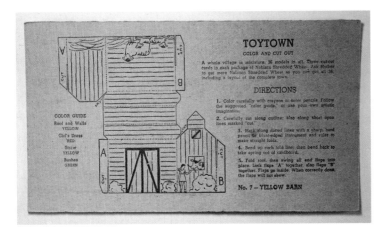

Nabisco Toytown yellow barn #7. $1-2-3

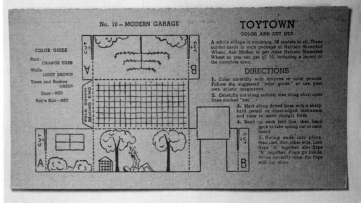

Nabisco Toytown modern garage #10. $1-2-3

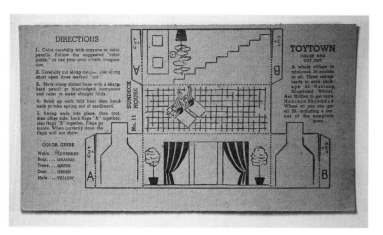

Nabisco Toytown sundeck house #11. $1-2-3

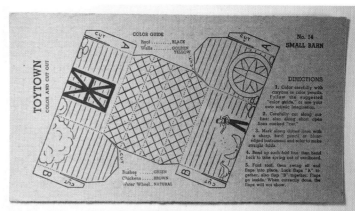

Nabisco Toytown small barn #14. $1-2-3

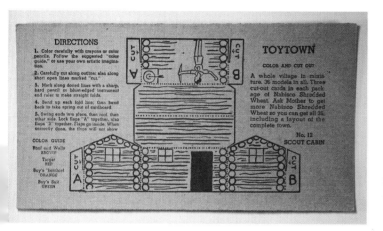

Nabisco Toytown scout cabin #12. $1-2-3

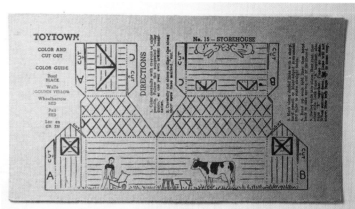

Nabisco Toytown storehouse #15. $1-2-3

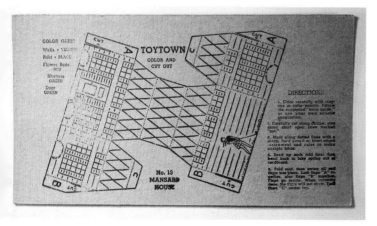

Nabisco Toytown Mansard house #13. $1-2-3

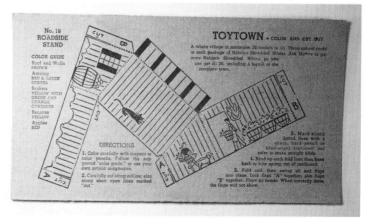

Nabisco Toytown roadside stand #16. $1-2-3

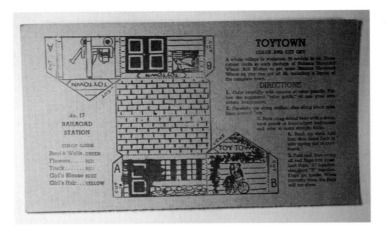

Nabisco Toytown railroad station #17. $1-2-3

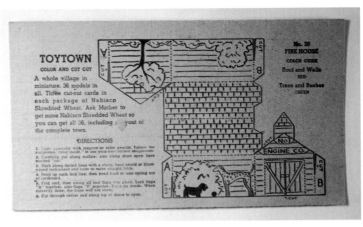

Nabisco Toytown fire house #20. $1-2-3

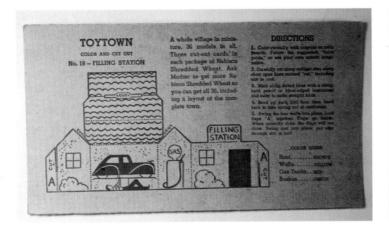

Nabisco Toytown filling station #18. $1-2-3

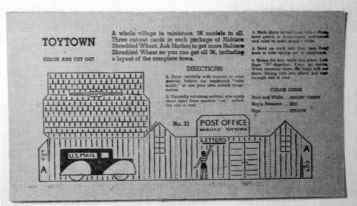

Nabisco Toytown post office #21. $1-2-3

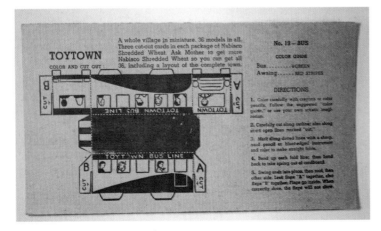

Nabisco Toytown bus #19. $1-2-3

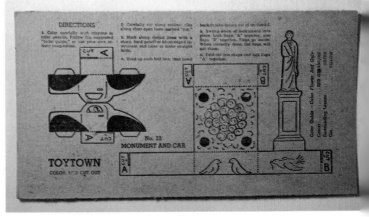

Nabisco Toytown monument and car #22. $1-2-3

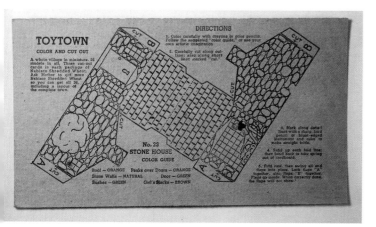

Nabisco Toytown stone house #23. $1-2-3

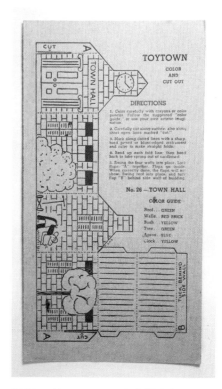

Nabisco Toytown town hall #26. $1-2-3

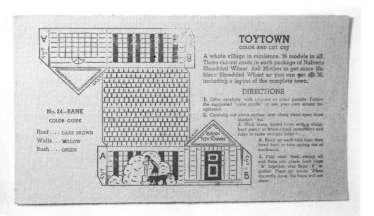

Nabisco Toytown bank #24. $1-2-3

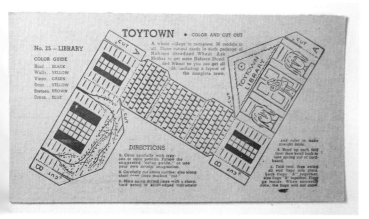

Nabisco Toytown library #25. $1-2-3

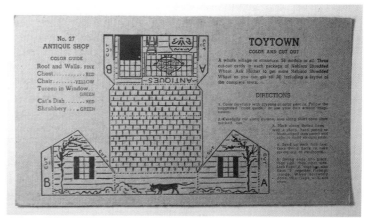

Nabisco Toytown antique shop #27. $1-2-3

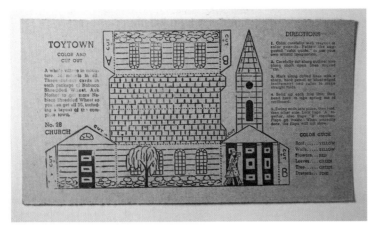

Nabisco Toytown church #28. $1-2-3

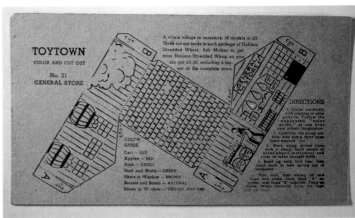

Nabisco Toytown general store #31. $1-2-3

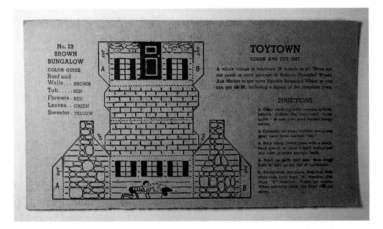

Nabisco Toytown brown bungalow #29. $1-2-3

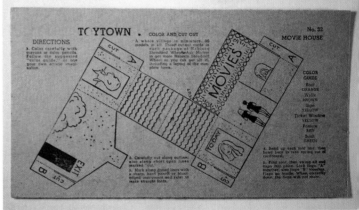

Nabisco Toytown movie house #32. $1-2-3

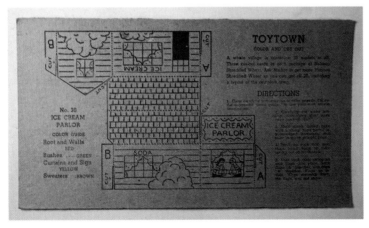

Nabisco Toytown ice cream parlor #30. $1-2-3

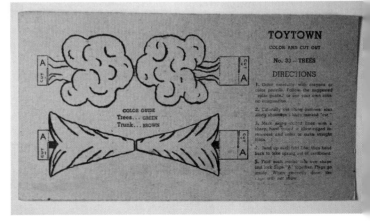

Nabisco Toytown trees #33. $1-2-3

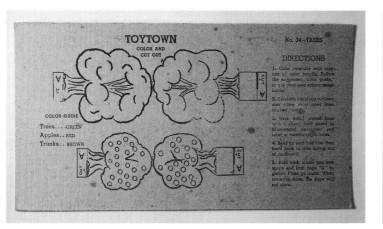

Nabisco Toytown trees #34. $1-2-3

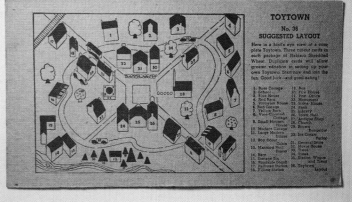

Nabisco Toytown suggested layout #36. $1-2-3

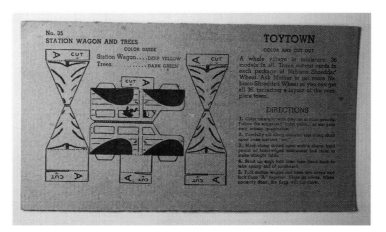

Nabisco Toytown station wagon and trees #35. $1-2-3

Toytown Carnival

There were 12 cereal biscuits to a box with 3 separator cards in each box. There were 36 cards to the Toytown Carnival set. You were to color the carnival pieces by using the color guide and then cut them out and put them together. A complete set is valued as follows: $50 (Good)-$75 (Fine)-$100 (Mint).

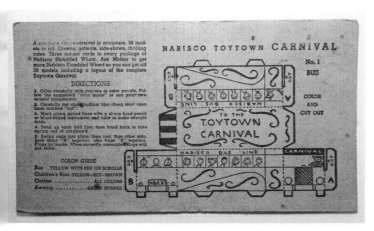

Nabisco Toytown Carnival bus #1. $1-2-3

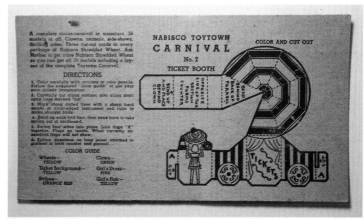

Nabisco Toytown Carnival ticket booth #2. $1-2-3

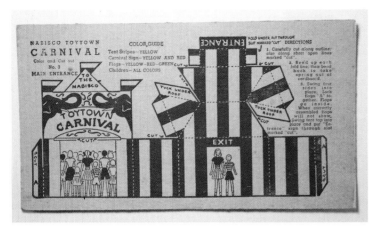

Nabisco Toytown Carnival main entrance #3. $1-2-3

Nabisco Toytown Carnival circus ring #6. $1-2-3

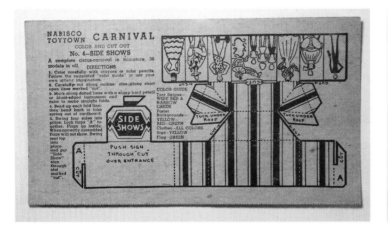

Nabisco Toytown Carnival side shows #4. $1-2-3

Nabisco Toytown Carnival tilting clown #7. $1-2-3

Nabisco Toytown Carnival cotton candy #5. $1-2-3

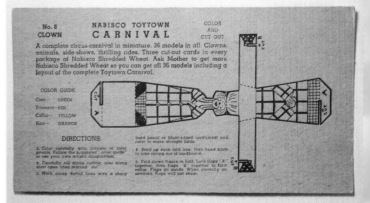

Nabisco Toytown Carnival clown #8. $1-2-3

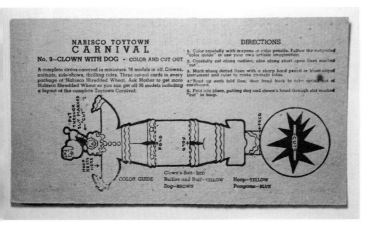

Nabisco Toytown Carnival clown with dog #9. $1-2-3

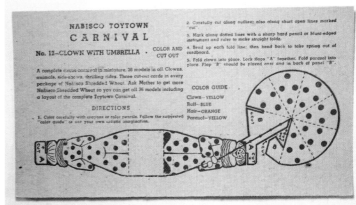

Nabisco Toytown Carnival clown with umbrella #12. $1-2-3

Nabisco Toytown Carnival performing horses #10. $1-2-3

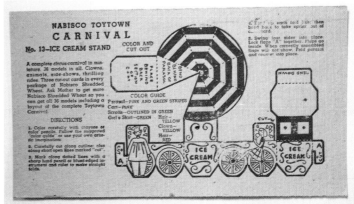

Nabisco Toytown Carnival ice cream stand #13. $1-2-3

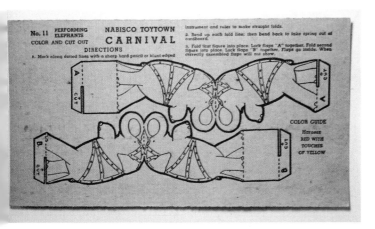

Nabisco Toytown Carnival performing elephants #11. $1-2-3

Nabisco Toytown Carnival fortune teller #14. $1-2-3

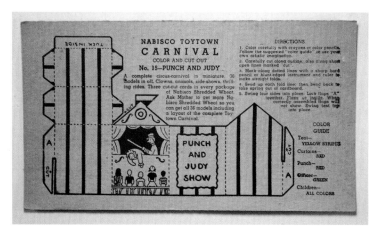

Nabisco Toytown Carnival Punch and Judy #15. $1-2-3

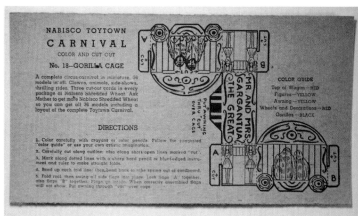

Nabisco Toytown Carnival gorilla cage #18. $1-2-3

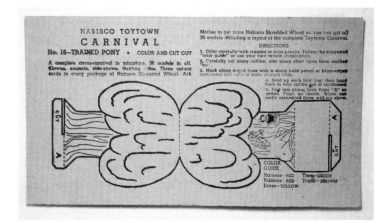

Nabisco Toytown Carnival trained pony #16. $1-2-3

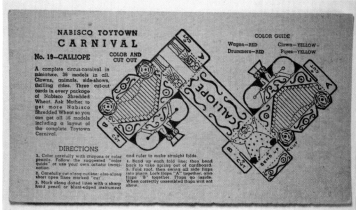

Nabisco Toytown Carnival calliope #19. $1-2-3

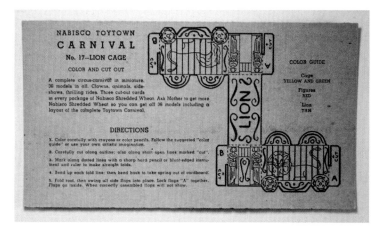

Nabisco Toytown Carnival lion cage #17. $1-2-3

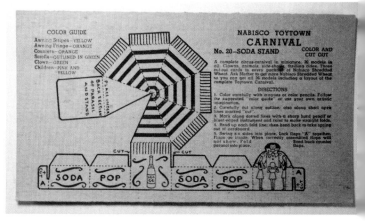

Nabisco Toytown Carnival soda stand #20. $1-2-3

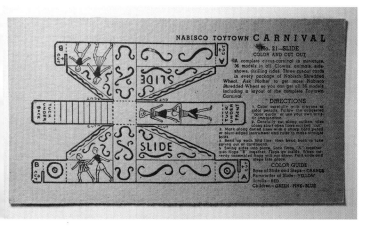

Nabisco Toytown Carnival slide #21. $1-2-3

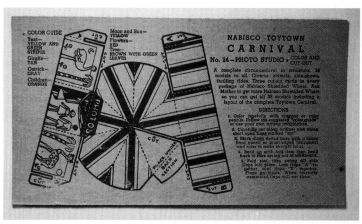

Nabisco Toytown Carnival photo studio #24. $1-2-3

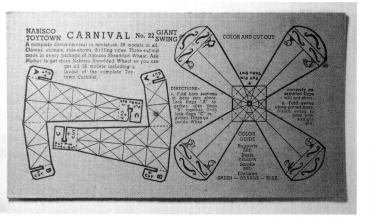

Nabisco Toytown Carnival giant swing #22. $1-2-3

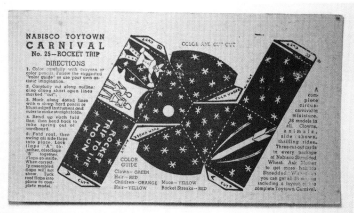

Nabisco Toytown Carnival rocket trip #25. $1-2-3

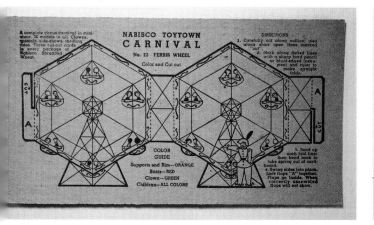

Nabisco Toytown Carnival Ferris wheel #23. $1-2-3

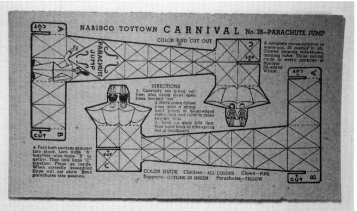

Nabisco Toytown Carnival parachute jump #26. $1-2-3

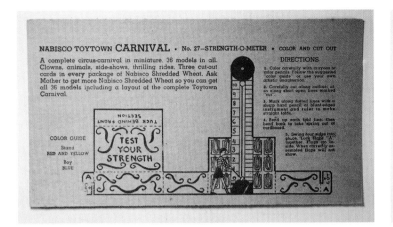

Nabisco Toytown Carnival strength-o-meter #27. $1-2-3

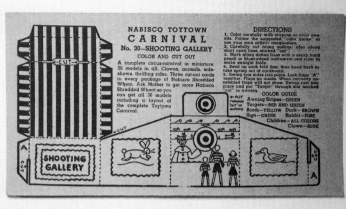

Nabisco Toytown Carnival shooting gallery #30. $1-2-3

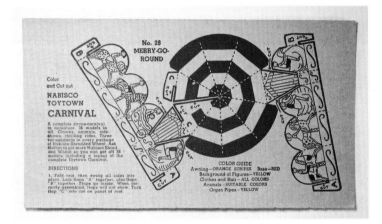

Nabisco Toytown Carnival merry-go-round #28. $1-2-3

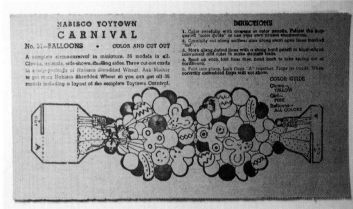

Nabisco Toytown Carnival balloons #31. $1-2-3

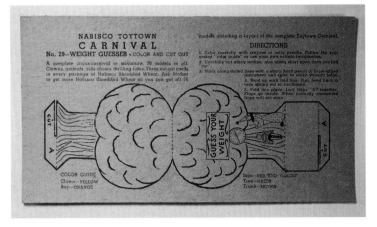

Nabisco Toytown Carnival weight guesser #29. $1-2-3

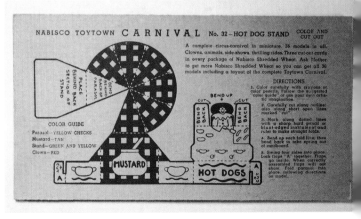

Nabisco Toytown Carnival hot dog stand #32. $1-2-3

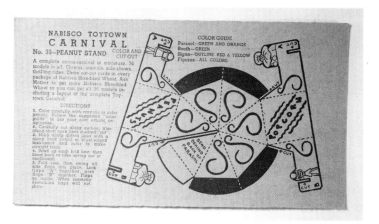

Nabisco Toytown Carnival peanut stand #33. $1-2-3

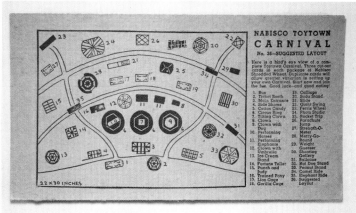

Nabisco Toytown Carnival suggested layout #36. $1-2-3

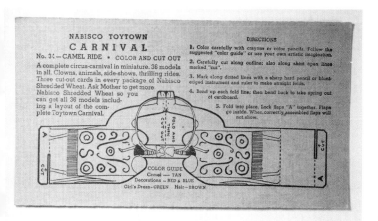

Nabisco Toytown Carnival camel ride #34. $1-2-3

Nabisco cover, Tony Sarg's animal circus. You were to color the pictures of the animals. There were 35 cards in this set, individually worth $1 (Good)-$2 (Fine)-$3 (Mint). A complete set is worth $40 (Good)-$75 (Fine)-$100 (Mint).

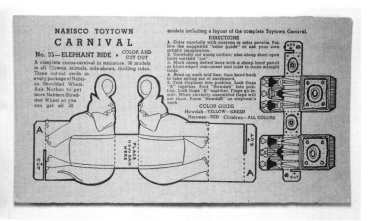

Nabisco Toytown Carnival elephant ride #35. $1-2-3

Nabisco cover, How America Travels. You were to color and cut them out. 36 cards to the set. $1-2-3 each; complete set: $40-70-110

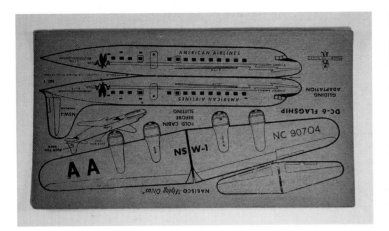

Nabisco Airplane from the Flying Circus. $5-10-15

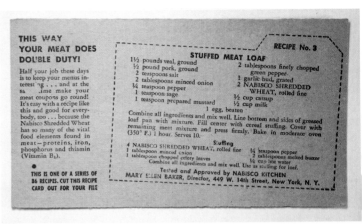

Nabisco recipes, 36 to the set. $ .50-.75-1.00 each; complete set: $20-30-40

Nabisco Picture Story Album cover. $1-2-3

Nabisco Picture Story Album, #1 of 36. $1-2-3

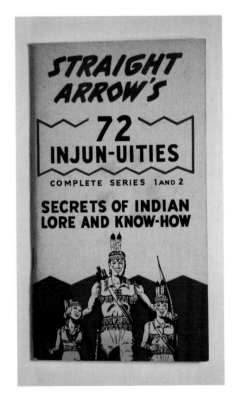

Nabisco Straight Arrow 72 Injun-Uities 1 and 2. This is a complete set of the Straight Arrow cards found in the boxes of cereal made in the 1950s. $40-50-60

Nabisco Rice Honeys Rin Tin Tin barrels of fun, 1"
long, made in 1956, whistle. $5-10-15

Nabisco Rice Honeys Rin Tin Tin barrels of fun,
1" long, made in 1956, skull. $5-10-15

Nabisco Rice Honeys Rin Tin Tin barrels of fun, 1"
long, made in 1956, compass. $5-10-15

Nabisco Rice Honeys Rin Tin Tin barrels of fun,
1" long, made in 1956, puzzle. $5-10-15

Nabisco Rice Honeys Rin Tin Tin barrels of fun, 1" long, made in
1956, deck of cards. $5-10-15

Nabisco Rice Honeys Rin Tin Tin barrels of fun, 1" long,
made in 1956, yo yo. $5-10-15

Post Cereal

Values by condition are in three classifications: Good, Fine and Mint.

Post rings made of tin in 1949, Maggie. $5 (Good)-$15 (Fine)-$20 (Mint)

Post Raisin Bran, star, 1950s. $5-10-15

Post rings made of tin in 1949, Sweet Pea. $10-20-30

Post rings made of tin in 1949, Captain. $10-20-30

Post Turbo Jet Pilot siren whistle, 3 1/2" long, made of plastic in 1949. $40-60-80

Post Toasties Yo Yo - Whistle - Puzzle - and Decoder, made in 1971. $40-60-80

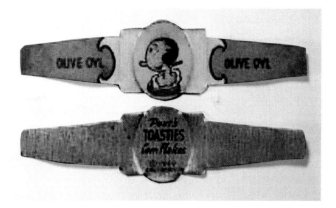

Post rings made of tin in 1949, Olive Oil. $10-20-30

Post Rodeo Stunt Rider, 1950s. $5-10-15

Additional Post Toasties Item:
Army Tank, plastic, 5" long, 1956. $40-60-80

Quaker Cereal

Values by condition are in three classifications: Good,
Fine and Mint.

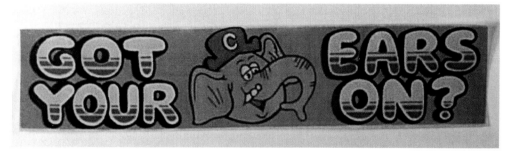

Quaker's Captain Crunch bumper sticker, 1970s. $1 (Good)-$2 (Fine)-$3 (Mint)

Quaker's Captain Crunch bumper sticker, 1970s. $1-2-3

Quaker's Captain Crunch bumper sticker, 1970s. $1-2-3

Quakers Captain Crunch bumper sticker, 1970s. $1-2-3

Quakers Captain Crunch bumper sticker, 1970s. $1-2-3

Quakers Captain Crunch ring whistle, 1970s. $5-10-15

Quakers Captain Crunch Bo'Sun whistle, 1970s. $5-10-15

Quakers Crazy Rings, 1950s, ship in a bottle. $20-30-40

Quakers Captain Crunch ring whistle, 1970s. $5-10-15

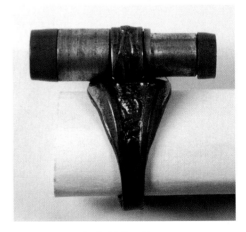

Quakers Pirate's Gold Ore Detector ring made in 1947. $50-100-150

Quaker Puffed Rice Gabby Hayes cannon ring, 1 1/2" long, made of various metal in 1951. $100-150-200

Quakers Gabby Hayes Movie Viewer, made in 1952. $100-150-200

Additional Quaker Cereal Items:

Shredded Wheat Sgt. Preston 10-in-1 trail kit	$75-100-125
Babe Ruth brass ring, 1934	$150-250-350
Captain Crunch fire truck, 1960s	$10-15-10

Quakers Shredded Wheat Sgt. Preston Aluminum Pedometer made in 1952. $60-90-125

Ralston Purina Cereal

Values by condition are in three classifications: Good, Fine and Mint.

Wheat Chex decoder ring, made of plastic and paper in the 1940s, scarce. $40-60-80

Ralston Purina Space Patrol hydrogen ray gun ring, made of plastic and metal in 1954. $150 (Good)-$200 (Fine)-$250 (Mint)

Ralston Purina Space Patrol metal buckle decoder made in 1951. $100-150-250

Ralston Purina Space Patrol metal buckle, back.

Trix Cereal

Values by condition are in three classifications: Good, Fine and Mint.

Trix Magic Number Cards made of cardboard in the 1970s. $3-7-10

Trix Whistle and magnifying glass made of plastic in the 1960s. $10 (Good)-$15 (Fine)-$20 (Mint)

Trix Magic Sword and Coin made of cardboard in the 1970s. $3-7-10

Trix Magic Color Cards made of cardboard in the 1970s. $3-7-10

Wheaties Cereal

Values by condition are in three classifications: Good, Fine and Mint.

Wheaties Moon Flower mask from the back of a Wheaties cereal box, made of cardboard in the 1954. Mask only: $50 (Good)-$60 (Fine)-$70 (Mint); complete box: $125 (Good)-$150 (Fine)-$175 (Mint)

Wheaties Pocahontas mask from the back of a Wheaties cereal box, made of cardboard in the 1950s. Mask only: $20-30-40; complete box: $60-70-80

Wheaties Bear mask from the back of a Wheaties cereal box, made of cardboard in the 1950s. Mask only: $5-10-15; complete box: $10-20-30

Wheaties Monkey mask from the back of a Wheaties cereal box, made of cardboard in the 1950s. Mask only: $5-10-15; complete box: $10-20-30

Wheaties Rabbit mask from the back of a Wheaties cereal box, made of cardboard in the 1950s. Mask only: $5-10-15; complete box: $10-20-30

Wheaties Elf mask from the back of a Wheaties cereal box, made of cardboard in the 1950s. Mask only: $5-10-15; complete box: $10-20-30

Wheaties Pirate mask from the back of a Wheaties cereal box, made of cardboard in the 1950s. Mask only: $5-10-15; complete box: $10-20-30

Wheaties Donald Duck mask, from the back of a Wheaties cereal box, made of cardboard in the 1950s. Mask only: $30-40-50; complete box: $80-90-100

Wheaties Goofy big game hunter comic book, made in the 1950s. $10-20-30

Wheaties Donald Duck and the Giant Ape comic book, made in the 1950s. $10-20-30

Wheaties Gus and Jaq Save the Ship, made in the 1950s. $5-10-15

Wheaties Grandma Duck Homespun Detective, made in the 1950s.
$10-20-30

Wheaties Sports Cereal Bowl, made in 1937. $50-60-80

Wheaties Lone Ranger Hike-O-Meter, made in 1957.
$50-60-70

Wheaties Sports Cereal Bowl.

Additional Wheaties Item:
Wheaties Pinocchio mask from back of
  Wheaties cereal box, cardboard, 1950s.
Mask only: $20-30-40
Complete box: $80-90-100

Wheaties Mini License Plates 1953

Wheaties mini license plates, 1953, are valued as follows: $3 (Good)-$5 (Fine)-$8 (Mint); Wheaties complete set of 1953 mini licenses plates: $250 (Good)-$350 (Fine)-$450 (Mint)

GA 53
E62-838
PEACH STATE

19 IOWA 53
76-9875
THE CORN STATE

0A·086
HAWAII

·KANSAS 53
TS · 4263
· THE WHEAT STATE ·

IDAHO 53
1R 9 622
WORLD FAMOUS POTATO

TOUR KENTUCKY ·'53·
886-101
BLAINE

ILL 1953
B32-486

3B 957
LOUISIANA · 1953

INDIANA
SB-7505
SB-7505 IND 53

MAINE 53
0404
VACATIONLAND

MASS 53
94-368

984-396
NEBRASKA 53

MICHIGAN
UT·36·66
53

38386
NEVADA 1953

10,000 LAKES
368·55
19 MINNESOTA 53

NH-53
A 0·248

MISSISSIPPI
212·484
OCT. WORTH 53

W N 27 R
N. 53 J.

THE TREASURE STATE
68-909
MONTANA 53

53 LAND OF ENCHANTMENT
0 34-75
NEW MEXICO

7J 98·70
NY·THE EMPIRE STATE·53

JUN. OREGON '53
661·35

752·860
NORTH CAROLINA 53

EXP. 3-31-54
1953 PENNA
PT040

NORTH DAKOTA i
328·66 1953

F86·04
RHODE 53 ISLAND

JU·1234
1803 - OHIO - 1953

SOUTH CAROLINA 53
I·8·12

OKLAHOMA-53
89·5440

1953 S.DAK
74·8933

Wheaties Mini License Plates, 1954

Wheaties mini license plates, 1954, are valued as follows: $3 (Good)-$5 (Fine)-$8 (Mint); Wheaties complete set of 1954 mini licenses plates: $250 (Good)-$350 (Fine)-$450 (Mint)

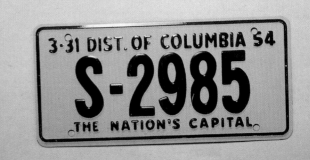

19 FLORIDA 54
68 W 7585
SUNSHINE STATE

54
AZ 2998
INDIANA

GA 54
P-96969
PEACH STATE

19 IOWA 54
73-9875
THE CORN STATE

0A·086
HAWAII

KANSAS 54
Z P-1234
THE WHEAT STATE

1 A 2 315
IDAHO 54

TOUR KENTUCKY·'54
989-431
WOODFORD

19 ILLINOIS 54
668 780
Land of Lincoln

777 333
19 LOUISIANA-YAMS 54

113

A·4201
SOUTH CAROLINA 54

E5672
54 VERMONT

S.DAK. 1954
64·4321

VIRGINIA 1954
987·232

95·9876
T.ENN. 54

1345JJ
54 WASHINGTON

TEXAS 54
PZ3579

425·634
W. VA. EXP.· 6·30·54

AM406
UTAH 1954

WIS JAN 54
F32·494
AMERICA'S DAIRYLAND

Wheaties mini license plate mailer, came with 12 mini license plates. $10-20-30

Dick Tracy

Dick Tracy started as a comic strip and became a radio program in the 1930s and 1940s. The sponsor was Quaker Puffed Wheat and Puffed Rice.

For membership, it took 2 box tops for the membership badge. For additional badges, you needed the following:

5 more box tops, a total of 7 for the Sergeant badge,
7 more box tops, a total of 14 for the Lieutenant badge,
10 more box tops, a total of 24 for the Captain badge,
15 more box tops, a total of 39 for the Inspector general badge.

If at some time you wanted to be a Patrol Leader, you had to turn in the names and addresses of 5 other kids, with 2 box tops from each (that's 10 box tops, plus 2 from you to get the Patrol Leader bar pin that's 12 more box tops). If you obtained all 6 badges, that's 51 box tops. Wow, that's a lot of cereal! That's so many box tops that we do not have a Patrol Leader bar pin to show. It would be worth: $150 (Good)-$200 (Fine)-$250 (Mint).

Values by condition are in three classifications: Good, Fine and Mint.

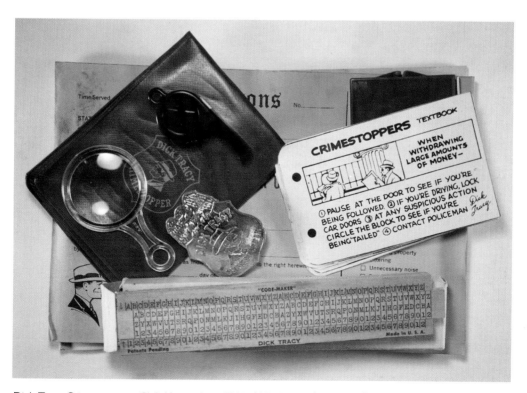

Dick Tracy Crimestoppers Club Kit made in 1961. $30 (Good)-$50 (Fine)-$70 (Mint)

Dick Tracy Air Detective wings badge made of brass in 1938. $40-$60-$80

Dick Tracy Sergeant brass badge, 1938. $80-120-160

Dick Tracy Member Secret Service Patrol 1 3/8" pin back by Quaker Cereals, made in 1938. $20-40-60

Dick Tracy second year member brass badge, 1939. $60-80-100

Dick Tracy Lieutenant badge, 1938. $100-150-200

Dick Tracy member brass badge, made in 1939. $40-60-80

Dick Tracy Captain, 1938. $100-200-300

Dick Tracy Inspector General, 1938. $300-450-600

Dick Tracy Girl's Division Badge, 1939. $20-30-50

Dick Tracy Secret Code Book, club manual.
$75-125-175

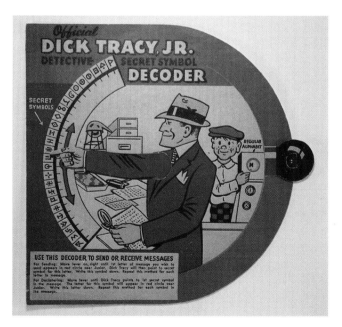

Dick Tracy 1944 decoder. $100-150-250

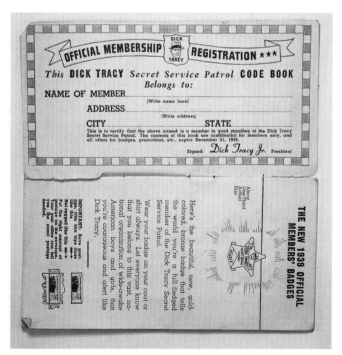

Dick Tracy Secret Code Book club manual, inside.

Dick Tracy button made in the
1930s. $20-40-60

Dick Tracy Crime Stoppers. $20-30-40

Dick Tracy movies in the box. $125-150-200

Dick Tracy Detective Club badge made in
1937 has leather cover on the back to wear
on your belt. $75-100-125

Dick Tracy movies, inside box.

Dick Tracy Detective Club badge back.

Dick Tracy film series for the Eugene Cine Vue, made in 1946. $20-30-40

Dick Tracy and Junior pocket knife. $40-60-80

Dick Tracy and Junior pocket knife, back.

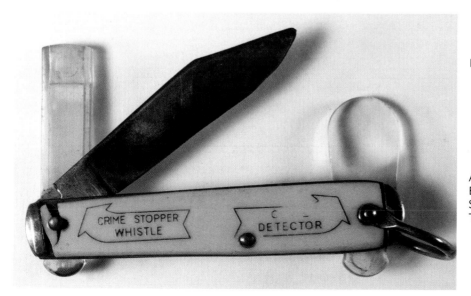

Additional Dick Tracy Items:
Enameled Brass Hat ring, 1930s $100-200-300
Secret Compartment ring, 1938 $200-300-400
The Big Little Book $20-40-60

G-Man Club

G-Man Club was on the Radio from the 1930s to the 1940s.

Values by condition are in three classifications: Good, Fine and Mint.

G-Man Ring. $10-15-20

G-Man Decoder made of cardboard, hard to find. $60 (Good)-$80 (Fine)-$100 (Mint)

G-Man Secret Operator ring made in 1937. $75-125-175

G-Man paper popper. $ 5-10-15

G-Man Badge. $20-30-40

G-Man siren whistle looks like the "Captain Marvel Power Siren" made in the 1940s. $50-100-125

The Green Hornet

The Green Hornet, sponsored by General Mills and Orange Crush, was on the radio through WXYZ Detroit, Michigan, from 1936 to 1952. It became a TV program from 1966 to 1967 on ABC.

Values by condition are in three classifications: Good, Fine and Mint.

The total set of nine pin backs carry the following values: $75 (Good)-$150 (Fine)-$200 (Mint) (not shown)

The Green Hornet Seal Ring Glow-in-the-Dark with secret compartment. $500-1000-1500

The Green Hornet pin back, made in 1966. $10-20-30

The Green Hornet pin back, made in 1966. $10-20-30

The Green Hornet pin back, made in 1966. $10-20-30

Jack Armstrong

Jack Armstrong was one of the longest running radio adventure serials, aired from 1933 to 1951.

Values by condition are in three classifications: Good, Fine and Mint.

Jack Armstrong Dragon's Eye ring made of white glow plastic in 1940. $400-800-1200

Jack Armstrong Magic Answer Box made of tin in 1938. $40 (Good)-$50 (Fine)-$60 (Mint)

Jack Armstrong Explorer Telescope made of cardboard in 1938. $20-30-40

Jack Armstrong Egyptian secret whistle made of brass in 1937. $50-100-150

Jack Armstrong Hike-O-Meter Pedometer made of aluminum in 1938. $50-80-125

Lone Ranger

The Lone Ranger aired as a radio program on WXYZ in Detroit, Michigan, from 1933 to 1955. The sponsors were Silvercup Bread, Bond Bread, Merita Bread, General Mills, Kix, Cheerios, and Wheaties.

Values by condition are in three classifications: Good, Fine and Mint.

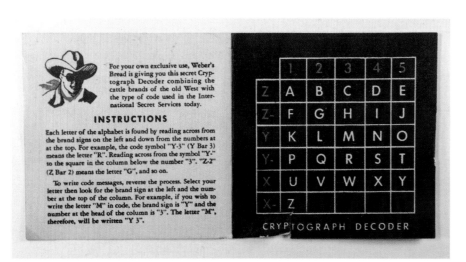

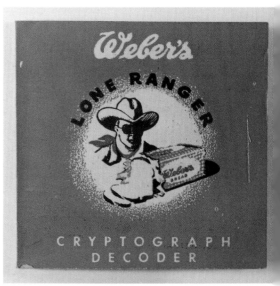

Lone Ranger paper Cryptograph Decoder by Weber's Bread made from 1943 to 1946, very hard to find. $150 (Good)-$250 (Fine)-$350 (Mint)

Left: Lone Ranger paper Cryptograph Decoder, inside.

Lone Ranger Good Luck token made from 1938-1940. $80-120-130

Lone Ranger Silvercup Bread Chief Scout badge made of brass in 1934. $100-200-300

Lone Ranger Bond Bread badge made from 1938 to 1940. $40-50-60

Lone Ranger Safety Scout Member's Badge made in 1934 by Silvercup Bread. $30-50-70

Lone Ranger Pocketknife, 1940s, red. $50-100-150

Lone Ranger Pocketknife, 1940s, white. $ 50-100-150

Lone Ranger silver bullet key chain pencil sharpener, 1 1/4" long, made of aluminum in the USA in the 1950s. $10-20-30

Lone Ranger plastic whistles made in the 1950s. $5-10-15

Lone Ranger silver bullet, aluminum, .45. The end of the bullet is marked LONE RANGER.

Lone Ranger silver bullet pencil sharpener, 1 1/8" long, made of aluminum by Clark MF'G CO. Orange VA in the 1950s. $15-35-40

Lone Ranger silver bullet, aluminum, .45, made from 1938 to 1940. $40-60-80

Lone Ranger silver bullet pencil sharpener, 1 1/4" long, made of aluminum by Clark MF'G CO. Orange VA in the 1950s. $10-20-30

Lone Ranger silver bullet, .45. Marked on the end is HI-YO REA A WAY.

Lone Ranger silver bullet, .45. Note: I have been told by many, many collectors that this was a Lone Ranger bullet. On the end is HI-YO REA A WAY. $10-20-30

Lone Ranger silver bullet, with a secret compartment and compass, made of aluminum in 1947. $60-80-100

Lone Ranger silver bullet opens.

Lone Ranger silver bullet, open with compass exposed.

Lone Ranger National Defenders Look Around ring made of brass in 1941. $100-125-150

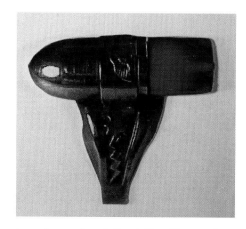

Lone Ranger Atomic Bomb Ring, Kix cereal in 1947. $50-100-150

HERE'S HOW YOU USE YOUR PEDOMETER

1. MEASURE YOUR STRIDE—Take several normal walking steps—then measure your stride from heel to heel. Read number on Pedometer dial closest to your stride. If stride is 25 inches long, read dial opening marked 25.

2. SET INDICATOR TO ZERO—With finger-tip, keep turning dial to right until zero is opposite small white markers. Do not turn past zero or you will have to turn dial all the way round again.

Lone Ranger Pedometer made of aluminum by Cheerios in 1948. $50-80-100

Lone Ranger Flashlight Ring made from 1947 to 1948. $50-100-150

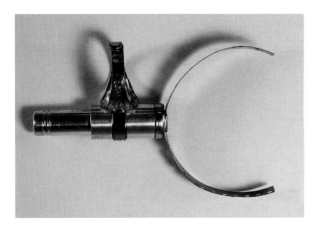

Lone Ranger Movie Film Ring with film, made in 1949.
$50-100-150

Lone Ranger film series for the Eugene Cine Vue, made in 1946.
$20-30-40

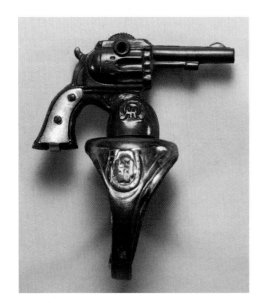

Lone Ranger Six Shooter, Kix cereal, made in
1948. $50-100-150

Lone Ranger National Defenders Danger-Warning Siren, made of plastic in
1941. *Courtesy of Janet M. Dundas.* Scarce. $300-600-1200

Lone Ranger picture by Silvercup Bread, made in
the 1940s. $30-40-50

Tonto picture by Silvercup Bread, made in the 1940s.
$20-30-40

Tonto picture by Silvercup Bread, back.

Lone Ranger kerchief made in the 1950s. $40-60-80

Lone Ranger picture by Silvercup Bread, back.

Additional Lone Ranger Item:
Bond Bread badge $20-30-40

Radio Orphan Annie

Radio Orphan Annie was a radio show from 1930 to 1942. You could join Annie's Secret Society until 1941 when it changed to the Secret Guard and then to the Safety Guard in 1942. Ovaltine sponsored the show until 1941 when Rice Sparkie's took over and then Quaker Puffed Wheat.

Of all the decoders that have been made throughout the years, the most famous of all has to be the Radio Orphan Annie 1940 decoder. This was the type of decoder that was used in one of the scenes in the movie *A Christmas Story*. The story was based on a young boy's desire to get a Red Ryder BB gun for Christmas and takes place in the 1940s. When this boy is asked what he would like for Christmas he says "I want a Red Ryder BB gun with a sun dial and a compass in the stock." People tell him that you will shoot your eye out.

Values by condition are in three classifications: Good, Fine and Mint.

Radio Orphan Annie's 1934 secret society manual. $60 (Good)-$80 (Fine)-$100 (Mint)

Radio Orphan Annie's 1934 secret society pin made of bronze. $20-30-40

Radio Orphan Annie's 1935 secret society round decoder pin. $60-70-80

Radio Orphan Annie's 1935 secret society decoder manual. $60-80-100

Radio Orphan Annie's 1936 secret society decoder manual. $60-80-100

Radio Orphan Annie's 1937 secret society decoder manual. $60-80-100

Radio Orphan Annie's 1936 secret society secret compartment decoder pin. $100-150-200

Radio Orphan Annie's 1937 secret society sunburst decoder pin. $60-70-80

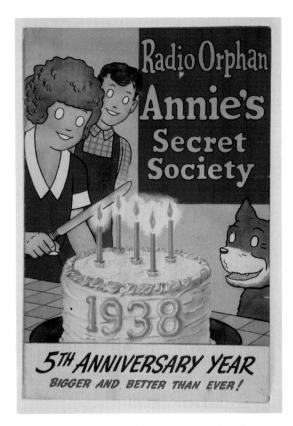

Radio Orphan Annie's 1938 secret society decoder manual. $80-100-120

Radio Orphan Annie's 1939 secret society decoder manual. $80-100-120

Radio Orphan Annie's 1938 secret society telematic decoder pin. $60-70-80

Radio Orphan Annie's 1939 secret society mysto-matic decoder pin. $50-75-100

Radio Orphan Annie's 1940 secret society decoder manual. $100-125-150

Radio Orphan Annie's 1940 secret society speedomatic decoder pin, back.

Radio Orphan Annie's 1940 secret society speedomatic decoder pin. $100-125-150

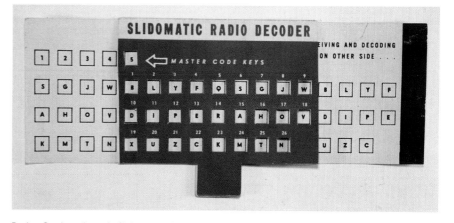

Radio Orphan Annie's Slidomatic decoder made of cardboard by Quaker Cereals in 1941. $75-125-150

Radio Orphan Annie's Code Captain brass buckle made in 1940, complete with belt. $200-300-400. Buckle only: $100-200-300

Radio Orphan Annie's 1930 Shake-up Mug type I. $70-80-90

Radio Orphan Annie's 1931 Shake-up Mug type II. $50-60-70

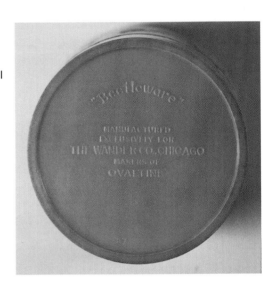

Radio Orphan Annie's 1931 Shake-up Mug type II, bottom.

Radio Orphan Annie's 1930 Shake-up Mug type I, bottom.

Radio Orphan Annie's 1930 Shake-up Mug, type I top.

Radio Orphan Annie's 1932 ceramic mug. $60-70-80

Radio Orphan Annie's 1933 plastic mug. $40-50-60

Radio Orphan Annie's 1938 Shake-up Mug. $150-175-200

Radio Orphan Annie's 1935 plastic mug. $60-70-80

Radio Orphan Annie's 1939 Shake-up Mug. $80-90-100

Radio Orphan Annie's 1935 Shake-up Mug. $80-90-100

Radio Orphan Annie's 1940 Shake-up Mug. $80-90-100

Ovaltine Shake-up, 7" high x 3 1/2",
made of aluminum in the 1940s.
$20-40-60

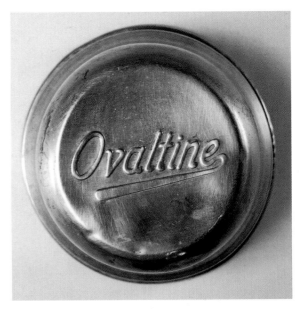

Ovaltine Shake-up, 7" high x 3 1/2", made of aluminum,
top.

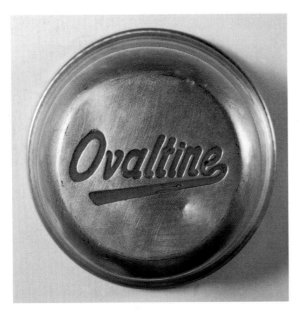

Ovaltine Shake-up, 7" high x 3 1/2", made of aluminum,
top.

Ovaltine Shake-up, 7" high x 3 1/2",
made of aluminum in the 1950s. $20-
30-40

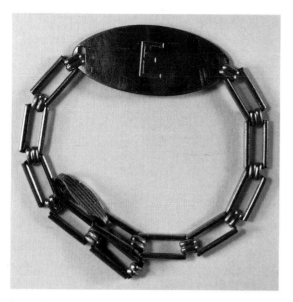

Radio Orphan Annie's 1939 identification bracelet.
$20-40-60

Radio Orphan Annie's 1934 lucky piece.
$20-30-40

Radio Orphan Annie's 1939 identification bracelet, back.

Radio Orphan Annie's 1942 tritone
signaller whistle badge. $60-80-100

Radio Orphan Annie's three-way dog whistle, Sandy's head.
$60-80-100

Radio Orphan Annie's 1941 mysto-snapper
membership clicker badge. $20-40-60

Radio Orphan Annie's 1938 sun dial watch.
$60-80-100

Radio Orphan Annie's 1938 sun dial watch, back.

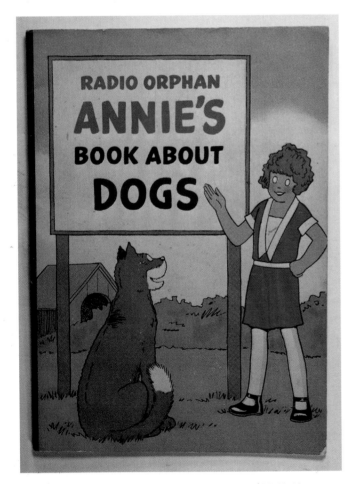

Radio Orphan Annie's 1936 *Book About Dogs*. $20-40-60

A 1936 *Ladies Home Journal* Ovaltine ad for mug. Note that the mug shown in the ad is a 1935 mug. $40-60-80

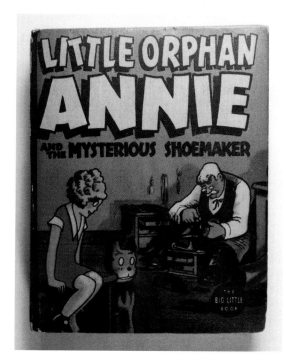

Radio Orphan Annie's 1938 *The Mysterious Shoemaker* by Big Little Books. $20-40-60

Radio Orphan Annie's 1947 *Gooneyville Mystery* by Better Little Books. $20-30-40

A 1936 *Ladies Home Journal* Ovaltine ad for a mug. Note that the mug shown in the ad is a 1935 shake-up mug. $40-60-80

A 1938 *Ladies Home Journal* Ovaltine ad for a mug. Note that the mug shown in the ad is a 1933 mug. $40-60-80

Radio Orphan Annie's 1930s gold color ring, Annie Face. $50-90-125

A 1939 *Ladies Home Journal* Ovaltine ad for a mug. Note that the mug shown in the ad is a 1933 mug. $40-60-80

Red Ryder

Red Ryder was on the radio from 1942 to 1949. One of the bread company sponsors was Langendorf Bread.

Values by condition are in three classifications: Good, Fine and Mint.

Little Beaver pinback made in the 1940s. $20-30-40

Red Ryder pinback made in the 1940s. $25 (Good)-$35 (Fine)-$45 (Mint)

Roy Rogers

Roy Rogers was on the radio from 1944 to 1955. Quaker Oats began offering premiums in 1948; Post Cereals continued the tradition when it took over in 1952.

Values by condition are in three classifications: Good, Fine and Mint.

Roy Rogers plastic mug by Quaker Oats made in 1950. $30-40-60

Roy Rogers Branding Iron Ring, with cap, made in 1948. $100 (Good)-$150 (Fine)-$200 (Mint)

Roy Rogers Deputy Star Badge, with a whistle and secret compartment, made in 1950. $ 80-90-100

Roy Rogers Deputy Badge made of brass in the 1950s. $10-20-30

Roy Rogers Deputy Star Badge, whistle and secret compartment, back

Additional Roy Rogers Item:
Roy Rogers on horse, in silver, 1950s
$150-200-250

141

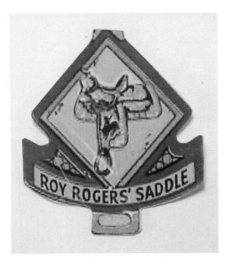

Roy Rogers Badge by Post cereal, made in the 1950s. $20-30-40

Sky King

Sky King was on the radio from 1946 to 1954. His sponsors included Peter Pan Peanut Butter and Power House candy bars. Sky King aired as a TV series from 1951 to 1966.

Values by condition are in three classifications: Good, Fine and Mint.

Sky King Magni-Glo Writing Ring, made in 1949. $50-75-100

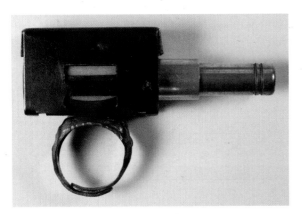

Sky King Tele-Blinker Ring made in 1949 by Peter Pan Peanut Butter. $50 (Good)-$100 (Fine)-$150 (Mint)

Sky King Magni-Glo Writing Ring, open.

Sky King Electronic Television Picture Ring made in the 1940s. $100-200-300

Sky King Spy Detecto Writer and Decoder made of aluminum in 1949. $75-125-175

Sky King Spy Decoder Writer and Decoder made of brass in 1949. $90-150-200

Sky King Navajo Treasure Ring made in 1950. $100-125-150

Superman

Superman was on the radio from 1940 to 1951, sponsored by Kellogg's Pep. It became a TV program in 1949.

Values by condition are in three classifications: Good, Fine and Mint.

Superman gum card. $5 (Good)-$10 (Fine)-$15 (Mint)

Superman Secret Code. This is a part of the Membership Kit, 1948. Complete kit: $175-250-500. Code folder only: $75-100-125

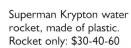

Superman Krypton water rocket, made of plastic. Rocket only: $30-40-60

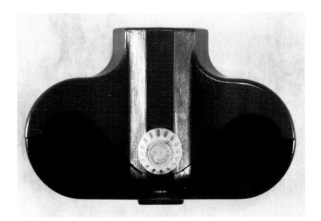

Superman, The Eugene Cine Vue, made in 1946. $50-100-150

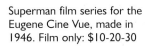
Superman film series for the Eugene Cine Vue, made in 1946. Film only: $10-20-30

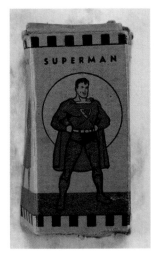

Superman, the Eugene Cine Vue, made in 1946, front.

Additional Superman Item:
Kellogg's Corn Flakes Superman
   rocket & launcher, plastic, 1955 $100-150-200

Tarzan

Tarzan was on the radio from 1932 to 1936 and again from 1952 to 1953. Post Toasties was one of many sponsors.

Values by condition are in three classifications: Good, Fine and Mint.

Tarzan Club Member Card, back.

Tarzan Club Member Card made in 1932. $150 (Good)-$250 (Fine)-$350 (Mint)

Tarzan member pin made in 1932.
$100-200-300

Tarzan Signal Club pin made in 1932. $50-75-100

Tarzan the Tiger pin. $200-250-300

Tarzan Jungle Tales viewer, 1940s. $60-80-100

Tarzan, Sons of Tarzan Club pin made in 1930. $50-
100-150

Tarzan, Big Little Book. $30-40-50

Tom Corbett, Space Cadet

Tom Corbett Space Cadet was on the radio in 1952 only and then went on to TV. The sponsor was Kellogg's Cereal.

Values by condition are in three classifications: Good, Fine and Mint.

Tom Corbett Space Cadet Ring, Kellogg's Pep Cereal, made of plastic in 1951. $40-50-60

Tom Corbett Space Cadet Decoder made in 1951. $50 (Good)-$100 (Fine)-$150 (Mint)

Tom Corbett Space Academy Ring, Kellogg's Pep Cereal, made of plastic in 1951. $20-30-40

Tom Corbett Space Cadet Decoder, back.

Tom Corbett Space Cruiser Ring, Kellogg's Pep Cereal, made of plastic in 1951. $20-30-40

Tom Corbett Parallo-Ray Gun Ring, Kellogg's Pep Cereal, made of plastic in 1951. $20-30-40

Tom Corbett Sound-Ray Ring, Kellogg's Pep Cereal, made of plastic in 1951. $20-30-40
There were 12 Tom Corbett, Space Cadet, Kellogg's Pep Cereal rings. A complete set: $200-300-400

Tom Corbett Space Cadet Kellogg's Cereal Flicker Disk made in the 1950s. $10-20-30

Tom Corbett Space Cadet Kellogg's Cereal Flicker Disk made in the 1950s. $30-40-50

Tom Corbett Space Cadet silver metal ring, made in 1952. $50-75-100

Tom Corbett membership pinback made in 1951. $75-150-200

Tom Corbett Space Cadet silver metal ring, made in 1952, side.

Tom Corbett Compass made in the 1950s. $100-150-200

Tom Mix

Tom Mix was a children's radio program from 1933 to 1950, sponsored by Ralston cereal.

Values by condition are in three classifications: Good, Fine and Mint.

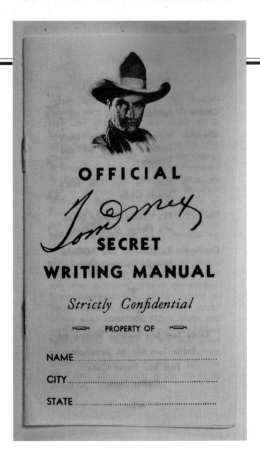

Tom Mix Secret Writing Manual made in 1938. $20-30-40

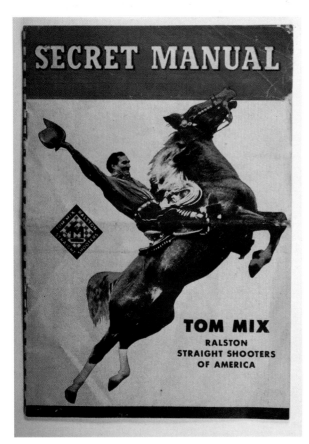

Tom Mix Secret Manual made in 1944. $40 (Good)-$70 (Fine)-$100 (Mint)

Tom Mix look-around ring by Ralston cereal, made in the 1940s. $100-125-150

Tom Mix felt patch, made in 1933. $75-100-125

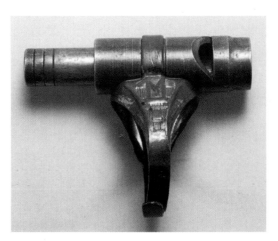

Tom Mix sliding whistle ring, made in 1949. $50-75-100

Tom Mix look-around ring, side.

Tom Mix nail ring, this is the same as the Gene Autry nail ring. $10-20-30

Tom Mix Championship belt and buckle, made in 1936. $100-150-200

Tom Mix six gun decoder, made in 1941. $100-125-150

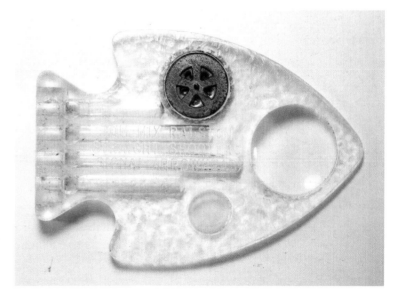

Tom Mix signal arrowhead, made in 1949. $50-75-100

Tom Mix Dobie County siren sheriff badge, made in 1946. $50-75-100

Tom Mix Straight Shooters Pocketknife, made in 1939. $50-80-120

Tom Mix Rocket Parachute, made in 1936. $100-150-200

Tom Mix gold ore watch fob, made in 1940. $50-75-100

Tom Mix gold ore watch fob, made in 1940, back.

Tom Mix glow-in-dark compass and magnifier, made in 1947. $50-75-100

Tom Mix Identification Bracelet, made in 1947. $20-40-60

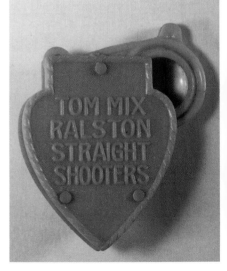

Tom Mix glow-in-dark compass and magnifier, made in 1947, back.

Tom Mix compass and magnifier, made of brass in 1940. $50-75-100

Tom Mix compass and magnifier, made of brass in 1940, back.